MY TIME WITH GOD

VOLUME 2

150 More Ideas for Your Own Quiet Time

MY TIME WITH GOD

VOLUME 2

150 More Ideas for Your Own Quiet Time

by
Jeanette Dall
Jean Gowen Dennis

Tyndale House Publishers, Wheaton, Illinois

Heritage Builders

MY TIME WITH GOD, VOLUME 2

ISBN: 1-56179-805-3

A Focus on the Family book published by
Tyndale House Publishers, Wheaton, Illinois.

Cover Design: Steve Diggs & Friends, Nashville

Illustrator: Gary Ciccarelli

For Lightwave
Concept Design and Direction: Rick Osborne
Managing Editor: Elaine Osborne
Text Director: K. Christie Bowler
Art Director: Terry Van Roon
Editorial Assistant: Mikal Clarke

Printed in the United States of America

01 02 03 04 05/10 9 8 7 6 5 4 3 2 1

CONTENTS

WHAT ARE TIMES WITH GOD AND WHAT'S THEIR POINT?

Is there a lot of noise in your life—telephone ringing, TV blaring, boom box booming, and computers buzzing and beeping? And how about the people coming and going—talking, singing, laughing, slamming doors, and rattling dishes? Maybe there's even a cat or dog making its own kind of noise and commotion. This is pretty normal for a busy family; maybe a family just like yours.

But there are also times that aren't so noisy and busy. These are times to sit and think or dream, maybe even make great plans for what you would like to do in the future. That's a good time to find a quiet corner and use this book. *My Time With God* will help you know what God is like and help you build a truly awesome relationship with Him.

You and God

It takes two to have a relationship. You get to know people by talking with them and sharing your thoughts and ideas. It's the same way with God. You can get to know God by spending time with Him and sharing your joys, sorrows, worries, and big ideas. *My Time With God* will guide you in developing this wonderful relationship through Bible readings, questions, prayers, and fun ideas.

Bible Readings

God speaks to you through the Bible. It is His love letter telling you about Himself and all the things He does for you. The Bible also shows you how to lead a life that pleases God. In *My Time With God* you will find verses to read in God's Word, the Bible, and interesting questions asking about what you have read. You can also learn how the Bible teachings have meaning in your life right now!

Prayers

You can talk to God through prayer. This is where you can share everything in your heart and mind with God. God is an excellent listener, and He always hears you. Better than that, God can always help you with your problems or worries. Do you sometimes feel like you don't know what to say? Don't worry. *My Time With God* will give you prayer starters and ideas to help you as you talk to your heavenly Father. But don't feel limited to those. In fact, add the prayer starters to the other things you pray about, such as friends and family, needs you know about, or requests for help on your tests. God wants to know all about what you care about and to help you with it all.

Fun Ideas

Good relationships are full of joy and fun. You will find some of that in *My Time With God*, too. You can chuckle at a joke, learn some way-out trivia, or figure out a riddle.

HOW DO YOU DO TIMES WITH GOD?

When and where can you spend quiet time with God? The answer is anytime, anywhere. Well, *almost* anytime. If you're in the outfield, the bases are loaded, the bat connects with the ball, the crowd goes wild in the stands, and you're running for all you're worth, you *can* still pray a quick prayer, but this is *not* the best time to open your Bible, sit down on the grass, and quietly listen to God.

A Special Place

Spending quiet time with God takes concentration; so you'll need to find a place where you can focus on Him and His Word. Many Christians call this time "devotions" because it's *devoting* time and attention to God.

A good time for it is first thing in the morning, before your day begins. But you can have quiet times in your backyard after school, on a hilltop, on a beach, 10,000 feet above the earth in a hot air balloon—just about *anywhere* ('cause God's everywhere)! If you don't own a hot air balloon, you can always go to your bedroom after supper. In fact, the Bible says, "When you pray, go into your room, close the door" (Matthew 6:6).

So where's your quiet place going to be where you can have a great time with God?

It's About God

In your special place, focus on God, realizing just how awesome He is. As Psalm 46:10 says, "Be still, and know that I am God." It takes *time* to get perfectly still, shove all the busy thoughts out of your mind, and focus your heart on God who loves you. So you might start with prayer. Remember, prayer is about a relationship with God. It's you talking to Him and Him responding to you. His response could be helping you understand the Bible or your situation, or giving you a sense of peace or a new way to deal with something. If things aren't quite right between you and God, get that taken care of.

When you've offended a friend, the first thing you need to do when you meet again is make things right. So check out your heart (Psalm 4:4; 139:23–24) and ask Him to show you anything in your life He wants to change.

Then open this book and your Bible. Reading the Bible thoughtfully and asking questions about what you read is a great way to focus on God. Not only do you learn interesting, amazing, and wonderful things, but as you read, your thoughts are on God and His ways—it becomes even easier to talk to Him. God uses the Bible (His book!) to speak to you and answer your questions, telling you how much He loves you and how much you need Him. Reading the Bible and praying are great steps toward giving God control over your thoughts and life. And that's what it's all about!

WHAT TO EXPECT AND
HOW TO USE THIS BOOK

The Bible is not simply a collection of scattered stories.
The writers of the Bible all contributed to tell one *big
story*. Down through history, from Adam and Eve in the
Garden of Eden to Christ on the cross, from Moses on
Mount Sinai to the apostle Paul in Rome, God has been
unfolding a special plan. *My Time With God* is designed
to help you see God's special plan for your life and to
give you hours of fun and interesting reading as you
draw closer to God.

About This Book

When you're comfortably seated in a corner with your
Bible, a notebook, and this book, you'll want to know how
the book works. *My Time With God* is divided into sections
for individual books of the Bible or a group of related
books. At the beginning of each section is a fun and
factual introduction explaining what that book of the
Bible or section is about. Read this introduction, then start
right in with your first day's reading.

The Starters

Each page or devotion helps you look at Bible stories from
several different angles. These are quiet time starters since
they get you started spending a quiet time with God.

At the top of the page, in the first few sentences, are
some Bible references. Be sure to look up and read those
verses in your Bible. Then look at *Think About It*. This gives
thoughts about your Bible reading and asks you questions
about what you've just read to get you thinking about it
and what it means to you. Take time to answer them,
because this is really what it's all about—finding out what
God's saying in His Word and then living it out.

Go Deeper is for those of you who want to read more about the story or the day's topic. It gives you other related Bible verses to look up.

Prayer Starter provides a suggestion to start your prayer time off with. Use this, but pray about other things too—such as your family and friends, and whatever is on your heart.

Facts and Fun is usually related to the topic, but sometimes just contains jokes, trivia, quizzes, and interesting information that's, well, just for fun.

Coming Up Next hints at what you'll find on the following page.

Your Choice

You can use this book in different ways. You can read it like we've just explained, or you can read it by topic. Say you want to learn about who Jesus is. Go to the *Topical Index* in the back of the book, look up "Jesus" alphabetically, then go to the page numbers listed and do those quiet time starters. You could also just choose a book you're interested in, say Daniel or Mark, and do those starters so that you get a good understanding of that book. If you get into a rut, check out *Different Ways to Have Time with God* or *An Index of Exciting Reads* at the back of this book. Whatever you choose, have fun and meet with God!

THE GREATEST STORY

The Bible tells one big story about God and His desire to have a wonderful relationship with us. It all began when only God existed—God the Father, Son, and Holy Spirit . . .

GENESIS-2 CHRONICLES

God made everything, including the first people, Adam and Eve. He gave them a beautiful garden to live in with only one rule: Don't eat fruit from a certain tree. Because Adam and Eve disobeyed God, however, He sent them out of the garden. Their sin separated them from God, and everyone born since then has also been born sinful and separated from God. The penalty for sin is death, but God had a plan to bring us back to Him. In the meantime, God told His people to sacrifice (kill) lambs to cover their sins.

About four thousand years ago, only a few people loved God. Job was one of them. He followed God even through tough times. Abraham loved God too. He was a man God chose for a special task. God sent Abraham to the land of Canaan and told him that He would give the land to his descendants forever.

Abraham's descendants, the *Israelites*, ended up as slaves in Egypt for 430 years. Finally they all left Egypt in one big "grand exit" called the *Exodus*. They returned to Canaan, conquered the land, settled in, and renamed it *Israel*. End of story? No.

PSALMS-SONG OF SONGS

The Israelites had some good kings like David and Solomon. They were so close to God that God spoke to them and gave them inspired messages to write down.

Some of these are in the Psalms where God made some amazing predictions called *prophecies*. He said that one day a descendent of David would become king. This king would be the *Messiah* (Savior) who would save Israel from her enemies. This Messiah would be no ordinary man, but the very Son of God Himself!

ISAIAH-MALACHI

After David and Solomon, most Israelites and Israelite kings forgot about God and worshiped idols. God began sending prophets (men and women with a message from Him). They warned the people that God would judge them if they didn't repent, but promised that He would bless them greatly if they would only serve Him.

Four of these prophets—Isaiah, Jeremiah, Ezekiel, and Daniel—are called *major* prophets because they had so much to say. And all of them gave wonderful prophecies about the coming Messiah. "God's got a plan, people! He's going to save you! Listen up!" But the Israelites didn't listen. God also sent other prophets. Twelve of them are called *minor* prophets because their books are short. But the Israelites didn't listen, no matter how much or how little a prophet said. So God judged them and allowed their enemies to take them as prisoners to distant Babylon. Did God give up on His people? No! His plan wasn't finished!

God raised up the prophet Daniel in Babylon. Daniel had fantastic visions about judgment, blessing, and—you guessed it—the soon-coming Messiah!

When the Israelites had been in Babylon seventy years and had repented, God allowed them to return to their own land. Now everything was ready for the key part of God's plan!

MATTHEW-MARK

Hundreds of years after the Jews returned to Israel, a young woman named Mary had a son named Jesus. Jesus was

God's own Son, the promised Messiah, but He became a person like us because He loved us. When He was about thirty, Jesus began to teach about God and His kingdom. He showed that God loved people by healing the sick and feeding the hungry, and He taught how to have a good relationship with God.

The religious leaders were afraid the people would follow Jesus instead of them, so they paid Judas, one of Jesus' disciples, to lead guards to Him. Jesus was arrested and tried for claiming He was God's Son, and then sentenced to be crucified. When He was nailed to the cross, Jesus, the ultimate "Lamb of God," died as payment for our sins.

After Jesus died, He was buried in a tomb. But on the third day the tomb was empty! Jesus appeared to many of His disciples, proving that He was alive again! This was God's plan all along to bring us back to Him so we could be His children again.

1 CORINTHIANS-JUDE

Jesus sent the Holy Spirit to help His disciples tell the world about Him, and men like Paul traveled all over, preaching the good news. The Greek word for Messiah is *Christ*, and soon the disciples became known as *Christians*. Several of Jesus' closest disciples—*apostles*—wrote letters to help these new Christians. Their letters are called epistles. Peter, Paul, and John wrote the most *epistles*, but James and Jude also penned some short, powerful letters.

REVELATION

The apostle John lived the longest and wrote the very last book in the Bible. When he was an old man and a prisoner on the island of Patmos, God gave him an awesome *revelation* (vision) about the return of the Messiah—Jesus—the end of the world, and the final glorious kingdom of heaven on earth when we would truly be with God again!

Have you ever heard a "rags to riches" story about a person who started out very poor but eventually became rich and powerful? Well, that's nothing compared to the story of Job! Job went from "riches to rags" almost overnight. He lost his riches, his family, and even his health. And guess who was behind all this mess—Satan himself!

And worse, some of Job's friends tried to convince him it was all his own fault. Some friends! They should have been comforting him. Sit down in the ashes with miserable suffering Job and hear what he and his "friends" have to say about God. You'll be surprised by a truly awesome ending to the story of Job!

Could Job have written this book?

Although most of the book of Job is the conversations of Job and his three friends, Job is not the author. The author was probably an Israelite. It could have been Moses, Solomon, Isaiah, Hezekiah, or Baruch (the prophet Jeremiah's assistant) but nobody knows for sure. We do know that no matter who the author was, God told him what to write.

We're not certain when the book of Job was written either. It tells of events which probably took place during the time of Genesis 12–50 when Abraham and his sons, grandsons, and great-grandsons were alive. Some people think the story of Job was told from generation to generation and put into writing long after the events took place.

Why tell such a sad story?

The writer tells Job's story in a way that helps us identify with how Job is feeling about what is happening. Even though Job loses everything, he never loses his trust in God. The message of the book of Job is that we don't always know why bad things happen. But no matter what happens, we can be sure that God loves us, and He is always in control.

NOW YOU SEE IT— NOW YOU DON'T

Have you ever had things just moving along perfectly—and then WHAM! everything turned awful? Even if it was horrible it was probably nothing like what happened to a guy called Job. Read Job 1:1–19, 22; 42:10–13 for the story.

Think About It
- Why was Satan against Job? Why do you think God let Satan attack Job?
- Job had an unbelievably rotten day! How would you have felt? How do you react when everything goes wrong?
- God had a plan for Job's life, and even though things went very wrong for a while (less than a year), God blessed Job again. God has a plan for your life too. How can knowing that help you get through rough times?

Go Deeper
Read Job 2:1–10; Matthew 5:10; Acts 14:21–22; James 5:10–11.

Prayer Starter
God always hears your prayers—tell Him about your life. Make two lists—one of the good things in your life and one of the bad things. Thank God for the good things and ask for His help with the not-so-good things.

Facts and Fun
Imagine being a millionaire and keeping your money in a field. That's what Job did! His wealth was in his animals, not a bank. So when he lost them he was flat broke.

Coming Up Next:
When is it not good to have friends around? When you're down in the dumps and they come along and make you feel worse! Meet some "friends" like that . . . next time!

HEY, MAN! WHAT DID YOU DO?

Imagine that you found your best friend covered with oozing sores from head to toe and sitting in a pile of ashes. What would you do? Read Job 2:11–3:1; 4:1–9; 11:1–6; 16:1–5 to find out what Job's friends did.

Think About It
- What would you have been thinking about for seven silent days if you had been there? Why did Job's friends think he was having all these problems?
- How did Job feel about what they said? How could they have been better friends?
- Jesus wants to be your best friend. What kind of a friend do you think Jesus is when you go through a tough time?
- Think of someone who needs your friendship. How can you be a real friend to that person?

Go Deeper
Read Job 15:1–6; 19:21–22; Proverbs 17:17; 18:24.

Prayer Starter
Friends shouldn't judge each other. They should listen, comfort, and help. Ask for God's help in being a real friend to someone who needs a friend. Pray for that person.

Facts and Fun
A friend who talks by the mile and listens by the inch should be removed to the yard.

Coming Up Next:
When everything goes wrong, it has to be somebody's fault, right? Who do you blame? See what Job has to say . . . next time!

NOBODY LOVES ME, EVERYBODY HATES ME!

Q: How can you get rid of "fair weather" friends? A: Have a storm of difficult things in your life. That's what happened to Job. But one friend still stuck around. Read Job 1:20–22; 2:9–10; 19:6, 11–27 for the rest of the story.

Think About It

- How would you have reacted if you were Job? Honestly, how does his response compare to yours?
- It's easy to blame God for troubles, but problems get worse when we turn away from Him. Even with all his troubles, how could Job keep trusting God? Is it easy to be like Job? Why or why not?
- Have you ever blamed God for your troubles? What happened?
- Why can you always trust God? Name three things you can trust Him for.

Go Deeper

Read Job 10:1–18; 13:15; Psalm 4:5; Proverbs 3:5–6.

Prayer Starter

Read Psalm 13 to God as a prayer today.

Facts and Fun

Knock, knock! *Who's there?*
Wire. *Wire, who?*
Wire you looking at me like that?

Coming Up Next:

What have a desert storm, science, and unlimited power got to do with Job? Learn about all these things . . . next time!

HOW BIG IS GOD?

Thunderbolts, lightning flashes, blizzards, floods, and hurricanes! What do you do when one of these comes roaring your way? Read Job 37:1–24 to find out more about these awesome displays of power.

Think About It
- What can you add to Job's friend's description of God?
- Job's friend, Elihu, described God's power and majesty. Then he got on Job's case for questioning God. Do you think he was right? Why or why not?
- How does God show His awesome power in nature? What does this tell you about Him?
- God is everywhere, knows everything, and can do anything. How can knowing that make you feel better when you're going through a tough time?

Go Deeper
Read Job 9:1–10; 26:6–14; Psalm 19:1–6; Romans 1:20.

Prayer Starter
Find a quiet place outside to pray today or sit by a window. Look around and praise God for His creation and power.

Facts and Fun
In Romans 11:34, Paul talks about the trouble with trying to figure out God. To find out what he says, make the following changes in the sentence: Z to A; Q to E; P to I; C to N; Y to O.

Why hzs kcywc thq mpcd yf thq Lyrd?

Coming Up Next:
If you could do absolutely anything you wanted for a whole month, what would it be? Listen to what a very famous person says he would do . . . next time!

Ever feel like shouting for joy, crying in frustration, or whimpering in fear? Are you sometimes "up," sometimes "down," and sometimes just there? Then this is the book for you!

The book of Psalms can help you express how you feel. You can clang cymbals, play drums, dance, and sing as you praise God for getting you out of a jam. But what can you say when you feel like God has forgotten about you? Whatever you feel—joy, anger, sorrow, or peace—you'll find those feelings written about somewhere in the Psalms.

Tough *and* sensitive? What a man!

Imagine a man who is a giant slayer, a courageous and hard-fighting soldier, and a mighty king. Then think about a man who is a dancer, singer, and talented musician. Could these men be friends? Well, they are even closer than that. They are both rolled up into one person, David.

Seventy-three of the psalms were either written by David or about David. Asaph, the Sons of Korah, Solomon, Moses, and others also wrote psalms. But 51 psalms don't have the names of the writers listed, so it's not clear who wrote them.

These psalms were written over a period of 850 years—from the time of Moses to the time of the Babylonian captivity. Talk about a long time in the making!

How's that tune go again?

Some of the writers may have originally written their psalms for their personal singing or praying. Others were written for group singing. Some were even written for soldiers to sing while marching into battle! Eventually the psalms were collected into one book and used for worship, praise, and confession to God.

The psalms actually consist of poems, prayers, and songs to God. You can think of the psalms sort of as a diary where people write about their deepest feelings toward God. Just as the writers tell God exactly what they are feeling, we can tell God exactly how we feel too. God always listens and promises to help.

HAPPY, THANKFUL, AND HAVING FUN

Think of your very favorite thing to do—something you do whenever you have some free time. How do you feel when you are doing this favorite thing? Read Psalm 1; 119:1–18 to find out what made the psalm writer happy.

Think About It
- Chaff is the seed covering and other "junk" removed from grain. It is worthless and blows away in the wind. How can you be sure that you are like a solid tree and not like chaff?
- Think about the kids you hang out with and the things that are most important to you. Are your friends helping you "be more like Jesus" or are they pulling you back? Why?
- The psalm writer loved studying God's Word and following what it taught. What do you like about the Bible? How can what you read today change your thinking?

Go Deeper
Read Deuteronomy 32:45–47; Psalm 119:19–48; Isaiah 56:2; 1 John 3:9.

Prayer Starter
The psalm writer used the word "blessed" several times to describe a person who loves God. Think of two ways you are blessed or two ways your life is good because you love God. Thank Him for them.

Facts and Fun
Knock, knock! *Who's there?*
Psalm. *Psalm, who?*
Psalmbody important.

Coming Up Next:
Can you predict what will happen next year, next week, tomorrow, or even an hour from now? Probably not. But learn about a true, astonishing prediction . . . next time!

TREATED LIKE A WORM

Could something you're going through now feel the same as what someone goes through 1,000 years from now? Can history repeat itself? Read Psalm 2:7–12; 22:1–18 for the story.

Think About It

- Why is David desperately praying for God's help? What would you have done in his situation? Honestly now!
- Psalm 22 tells about David's troubles, and about something that was to happen to Jesus hundreds of years later. What do you think it is? (Check out Matthew 27:35–50.)
- David probably wrote down how he felt at the time and, in the process, told about what would happen to Jesus. Who do you think helped David write about the future? How does that help you know the Bible is true? How can that help you trust God?

Go Deeper

Read Psalm 2:1–6; Matthew 27:33–46; Acts 4:23–28.

Prayer Starter

David wasn't afraid to tell God how he felt. He was always respectful, but he spoke to Him out of his heart. Spend some time telling God how you feel right now about your life.

Facts and Fun

Even though the psalms were written long before Jesus was born, many of them seem to describe Jesus the Messiah (Christ, the "anointed one") as much as they did things that were happening at the time the psalm was written. Jesus Himself often quoted from the book of Psalms. Many things that happened at Jesus' crucifixion and many of His words on the cross are predicted in Psalms.

Coming Up Next:

Look at the sky and everything in it, and then look at yourself. How are you the same? Don't get it? You will! Learn the answer . . . next time!

GOD'S AUTOGRAPH

Authors sign their books, artists put their signatures on their art, and we write our names on things we make. Why? We want people to know what we created. Read Psalm 8; 139:1–16 to find out about the greatest Creator of all!

Think About It

- It's not just the signature on art work that shows who the artist is, it's also the artist's style and technique. Things like beauty, order, and detailed design show God is creation's artist. Name several awesome things in creation that show God's "signature."
- God created the whole universe and He created you. Which is more important to God? How do you know?
- God knows absolutely everything about you, tons more than you know yourself—and not just because He knows everything but because He cares. How does that amazing fact make you feel? Why? How does it make you want to act?

Go Deeper

Read Genesis 1:26–28; Psalm 19:1–6; 33:5–15; Romans 1:20.

Prayer Starter

Make a list of ten good things about yourself. Then thank God for making you that way and for taking care of you.

Facts and Fun

Sam said to his friend, "I think I was put together backwards."

James asked, "Really? What do you mean?"

"Well, my feet smell and my nose runs," Sam explained.

Coming Up Next:

Ever feel like you need armor to protect you from mean kids? Learn about someone else who needed protection big time . . . next time!

NO NEED TO BE SHEEPISH

Who scares you? Is it the school bully or kids who make fun of you or just "bad guys" in the neighborhood? Ever feel like it would be nice to have someone walk beside you, stick up for you, and look after you? Read Psalm 23:1–6 and 27:1–14.

Think About It
- Imagine being the sheep in Psalm 23. What would it feel like?
- Of course God doesn't want us to be sheep. But He wants to walk along with us and care for us like a shepherd does his sheep. How is God like a good shepherd? Sheep will follow their shepherd. How are you like one of God's sheep?
- Why wasn't David afraid of the evil men who were his enemies? Why don't you need to be afraid?
- Think of a tough situation you've been through or are facing. Name two ways you can be like a sheep who depends on its shepherd.

Go Deeper
Read Psalm 3:1–8; 13:1–14:7; Matthew 6:25–27; 1 Peter 5:7.

Prayer Starter
Read Psalm 23 as a prayer.

Facts and Fun
Often shepherds in Bible days kept their flocks together. In the morning each shepherd would call his sheep. Each sheep recognized its own shepherd's voice, picked him out of all the others, and followed him! Whose voice do you recognize and follow?

Coming Up Next:
Ever been in a really tight spot where it looked like there was no way out? Then just in the nick of time someone rescued you. Whew! Learn about someone else who went through that . . . next time!

FEAR/GOD'S CARE

SOS

SOS (short for Save Our Souls) is a distress signal sent out when someone is in serious trouble. Anyone hearing it is supposed to come to the rescue. David sent out an SOS to God when he was in trouble in an enemy camp. Read Psalm 34:1–22 to find out if it was answered.

Think About It

- Imagine you're behind enemy lines and about to be discovered. What would it be like? What would you do?
- An enemy doesn't have to be a person and being behind enemy lines could be being right in the middle of a bad situation. How are you "behind enemy lines" or in need or rescuing in real life? How can you get help?
- "Fearing the Lord" means to *have respect* for God—not *to be afraid* of Him. How can you respect (fear) God? Name three good things or blessings (like peace or good friends) that can come from respecting God and trusting Him.

Go Deeper

Read Psalm 37:1–40; 42:1–11; Proverbs 3:5; John 14:1.

Prayer Starter

Write SOS on a paper and list some of your troubles or problems that you could use help with. Under the list write: "Trust in the LORD" (Proverbs 3:5). Pray to God about your top three troubles and trust Him to help you.

Facts and Fun

David was hiding but an enemy king recognized him. To protect himself, David pretended to be completely bonkers and did all kinds of crazy things. The king was disgusted and threw him out and David was safe (1 Samuel 21:10–15). He wrote this psalm of praise after that happened.

Coming Up Next:

Ever fallen in a mud hole? Yuck! Learn what David did when he was "in the pits" . . . next time!

THE SLIMY PIT

Imagine you are hiking all alone and all of a sudden you slip into a filthy, disgusting hole full of slime! Yuck! How do you feel? David speaks of that feeling. Read Psalm 40:1–17 and 125:1–5 and you'll see.

Think About It
- If you heard or read the words "slimy pit" what kind of a place do you imagine it to be?
- David's slimy pit, mud, and mire were made of troubles, being made fun of, and sin. What might make up your "slimy pit" (such as anger or disobedience)? How do you get caught in it? What three ways can you try to get out of it?
- David prayed to God and trusted Him for help, and then he always thanked God for His help. What is your reaction after God helps you?

Go Deeper
Read Psalm 71:1–24; 121:1–8; Matthew 20:28; Galatians 1:3–4.

Prayer Starter
Think of how God helps you. Write your own "psalm of praise" or thank-you note to God for rescuing you from your "slimy pit."

Facts and Fun
Many of David's psalms are about his terrible troubles or how God rescued him from them. What was often David's biggest problem? What kind of trouble did he have?

Find the answer by decoding the message below. Write the letter of the alphabet that comes AFTER the one given.

LZMX DMDLHDR VDQD SQXHMF SN JHKK GHL

Coming Up Next:
Get ready to shout and cheer at the top of your voice! Warn the rest of your family of possible loud noise violations before you read . . . next time!

NUMBER ONE!

Ever been to an exciting ball game with a close score? All the fans shout and carry on whenever their team makes a good move. They may even start yelling, "We're number one!" Read Psalm 47:1–9; 96:1–13, David's cheer for "number one."

Think About It

- Why did David think God was great? What do you think are the greatest things about God? Why?
- One of the ways David shared his joy and love for God was by writing a song and singing. How can you share your joy and love for God? Sing? Shout? Jump up and down? Go ahead, try it!

Go Deeper

Read Psalm 65:1–13; 135:1–21; Isaiah 66:23.

Prayer Starter

Along with the other things you pray about, thank God for His greatness and all the ways He has and will help you. Go ahead and be a little loud.

Facts and Fun

The church service was running long and people were getting restless. So the pastor decided to shorten the prayers. He said, "Dear God, you know our thoughts. Amen."

Coming Up Next:

Done something wrong? Miserable? Learn about someone who felt as if *everything* was wrong . . . next time!

YOU REALLY BLEW IT!

Have you ever had a TV or sports hero who did something really bad? Did they cry a lot and say they were sorry ? Read Psalm 51:1–19 for King David's "sorry" prayer.

Think About It

- How could David love God and still commit terrible sins? What do you think led to his sin?
- What leads you to sin and hurt God and other people?
- What can you do to please God rather than offend Him (or others)? (For example, think about how your actions or words might hurt someone.)

Go Deeper

Read 2 Samuel 11:1–27; Psalm 32:1–33:22; 38:1–22.

Prayer Starter

Do you need a reminder to tell God you're sorry for your sins and to ask for forgiveness? Try making this simple reminder—cut out a black circle and a bigger red heart with a cross on it. Think of the circle as a picture of sinful things you have done. Tell God that you're sorry for them and cover the circle with the heart. Then thank God for His love and forgiveness.

Facts and Fun

The Sunday school lesson was about the Prodigal Son. The class had talked about doing bad things and feeling guilty.

The teacher asked a girl, "Do you feel bad when you don't listen to your mom?"

The girl answered, "Yeah. But it makes my mom feel even worse!"

Coming Up Next:

Losing is not a lot of fun, but winning is great. Learn about victory over enemies . . . next time!

 **FORGIVENESS/SIN**

YOU LOSE!

How can you be a winner when it looks like you're losing? David was constantly on the run for his life. But David still felt he was the winner. Read Psalm 56:1–13 and 57:1–11 to find out why.

Think About It
- Put yourself in David's place. You have lots of enemies and they're attacking you in different ways. One wants to kill you, and lots of them want your kingdom. What are you (David) going to do?
- What do you think helped David keep going? What positive things could he have found in his situation? (For example, he wasn't dead yet! He had friends with him. . . .)
- You may not have any enemies like that but there are probably people or things that bother you. Maybe a kid picks on you or people around you use bad language. Name three other things that bother you. What do you do when things get really tough? (Cry? Pray?) How can you follow David's example?

Go Deeper
Read Psalm 46:1–11; 63:1–11; Joel 3:16; 1 Timothy 2:8.

Prayer Starter
Think of situations where it looks like you're losing—you're having trouble with math or you're always picked last for a game. Pray to God about them.

Facts and Fun
When can a shadow protect you from harm or enemies? *(Answer: When it's the "shadow of [God's] wings" [Psalm 57:1].)*

Coming Up Next:
Does it seem like everyone has better stuff than you do? Does it seem unfair? Learn what's fair . . . next time!

IT'S NOT FAIR!

Does it sometimes seem that being good just isn't worth the trouble? Do other kids seem to have more fun and get more attention than you? "It's just not fair!" Someone in Bible times felt that way too. Read Psalm 73:1–28 to find out about him.

Think About It
- What's the worst situation you have ever been in? What made it so bad? If Asaph had been there, what do you think he would have done? How can you be like Asaph?
- What are some things that seem unfair to you (for example, your friends can watch movies you aren't allowed to or you have more chores than your younger sister)? Think of two ways to change your attitude about what's fair.

Go Deeper
Read Deuteronomy 32:4; 2 Samuel 22:31; Psalm 15:1–5; 141:1–10.

Prayer Starter
Read Galatians 3:26–29. Thank God for treating all people the same and ask for His help in acting that way with the people in your life.

Facts and Fun
How do seven kids divide five potatoes fairly? *(Answer: Mash them.)*

What was the most successful thing ever invented? *(Answer: The postage stamp, because it always sticks to its job until it's completed.)*

Coming Up Next:
Imagine sitting on a rooftop with swirling flood waters below you; what do you do? Learn where David found help . . . next time!

SAVE ME!

What do people in a burning building and a sinking ship have in common, besides danger? They are probably all shouting, "Help! Save me!" Read Psalm 86:1–12; 116:1–7, 12–14 for David's shout to be saved.

Think About It

- Imagine yourself walking down a narrow alley. In front of you is a mean, snarling dog and behind you are some tough-looking bullies. Man, are you in trouble! What would you do?
- David always seemed to be in some kind of trouble, and he was always shouting, "Help! Save me!" Why do you think David kept turning to God when he was in trouble?
- Who do you ask to "save" you when you are in trouble? Can they truly help? Every time? Why or why not? Who should you turn to? Why?

Go Deeper

Read Job 22:27; Psalm 142:1–143:12; Isaiah 30:19.

Prayer Starter

What problem is really "bugging" you right now? Can you see a solution or a way out? Talk to God about it and ask for His help. Then thank God for His concern and love.

Facts and Fun

In many of the psalms David talks about enemies and being chased by those who want to kill him. During his life, David really *did* have lots of enemies who wanted to see him dead. Some of these were the giant Goliath, King Saul, a son of King Saul, the Ammonites (a nation that fought with Israel), and David's own son, Absalom.

Coming Up Next:

Finally! David's enemies were defeated! He could come out of hiding! Learn how David celebrated . . . next time!

SING, SHOUT, AND JUMP ABOUT!

Rivers clapping their hands? Mountains singing? Is David crazy? Read Psalm 98:1–9; 100:1–5; 138:1–8 to find out what he thinks could cause so much crazy happiness.

Think About It

- What would make you burst into song or do a jig of happiness? (Banning all vegetables? Going camping with a buddy? Receiving great news?)
- For David, knowing God loved him and could be counted on made him want to sing. Have you ever been really happy because of something God did for you? What was it?
- What would make worship at your church exciting? (Certain music? Your own band?)
- Worship is also our whole attitude of awe and thankfulness to God. Name three things you can thank God for that make your life exciting or that you're excited about.

Go Deeper

Read Exodus 15:1; 2 Samuel 6:12–15; Psalm 103:1–22.

Prayer Starter

Think of some unusual way you can show God you're excited about what He does for you. (For example, make your bed an Old Testament temple and hold your own service, stand on your head while making up a song. . . .) Then thank God for the things you're excited about.

Facts and Fun

Knock, knock! *Who's there?*
Sam. *Sam, who?*
Sam, the drummer. *Beat it.*

Coming Up Next:

Besides God, what's your very favorite thing in the whole world? Learn about David's favorite thing . . . next time!

PRAISE /WORSHIP

A LIGHT IN THE NIGHT

Have you ever camped in the woods on a dark night? You really need a flashlight or lantern. Without a light to guide you, you would soon be lost. Psalm 119:97–112, 161–168 talks about a light in the night too.

Think About It
- How can the Bible be like a light?
- Imagine the Bible is a lamp that guides you to help you know what God wants you to do and how He wants you to act toward others. What kind of things would it tell you to do? What good things can it lead you to? What dangers can it show you and lead you away from?
- If God's Word is the source of light like that then when we follow it we become like a light too. Name three ways you can be a light to your friends this week. (For example, you can be respectful to adults, tell the truth. . . .)

Go Deeper
Read Psalm 119:49–96; Proverbs 20:27; 2 Peter 1:19.

Prayer Starter
Turn off all the lights. Turn on a flashlight as a reminder that God's Word shows you the way to live. Thank God for His Word.

Facts and Fun
The lamps used in David's time were quite different from our bright lamps, flashlights, and lanterns. They were small bowls containing oil with a wick burning in it. These lamps gave just enough light to see a path. No reading under the covers with them!

Coming Up Next:
Sea creatures, lightning, wild beasts, and people all doing the same thing. What *are* they up to? Find out . . . next time!

NOTHING LASTS FOREVER

Have you ever heard the expression "Nothing lasts forever"?
People usually say it when something good is over. Or when
something breaks or wears out. Read Psalm 136:1–9;
148:1–14 to learn about something that *does* last forever!

Think About It

- Picture different plants and animals praising God. How
  might they do it (for example, a tree waves its branches,
  coyotes howl, etc.)?
- What reasons besides the ones in these psalms can you
  give for thanking and praising God?
- God's love endures forever—it never ends. Is that
  important to you? Why?
- Everything God created praises Him by being what He has
  made it to be. How can you praise God (for example, by
  developing the talents He gave you)?

Go Deeper

Read Psalm 145:1–146:10; 150:1–6; Matthew 6:25–34;
Romans 5:8.

Prayer Starter

Use Psalm 136:1–9 as your prayer today. Change the words
"His love endures forever" to a different phrase that tells
how you feel about God (like "He never leaves me" or "God
never changes"), and say it after each verse.

Facts and Fun

"His love endures forever" is repeated after each verse in
Psalm 136 because it was written for worship. Thousands of
people gathered together for worship. The leader would sing
the first part of the verse, and then the people would
respond, "His love endures forever."

Coming Up Next:

Want to be better than smart? Want to get "straight A's" in
life? Learn how in the book of Proverbs . . . next time!

GOD'S LOVE/PRAISE

PROVERBS & ECCLESIASTES

Ever had tired ears and an overloaded brain from all the things you're told to do or not do? It seems like everybody wants to give advice. Sometimes the advice is great and sometimes it's totally rotten! Knowing whose advice to follow can be downright confusing. Well, it's time to open up your ears and your mind for some wise advice from God Himself.

The book of Proverbs gives good advice on everything from managing money to friendship to how to treat others. You may find some of these proverbs and bits of wisdom funny and worthy of a chuckle or two.

The book of Ecclesiastes, however, has very little humor. Like Proverbs, it offers wise advice—but on a different subject and in a different way.

Who's the wise guy?

Proverbs are wise sayings. They tell us how we should act, and they help us understand everyday life. Who else would write it but Solomon, the wisest king to rule Israel? According to 1 Kings 4:32, Solomon "spoke three thousand proverbs." Not all of them are in the book of Proverbs. Agur and King Lemuel, two unknown men never mentioned anywhere else in the Bible, wrote some of the later sections of the book. Solomon wrote most of these proverbs in his early years as king. But the whole book may not have been completed until Hezekiah was king, over 200 years after Solomon died.

Most people think that Solomon also wrote Ecclesiastes—maybe when he was feeling "down." Others think that an unnamed teacher who lived some years after Solomon wrote it. If Solomon wrote the book, it was probably written around 935 B.C., late in his life.

What do you mean, "Money isn't everything"?

These two Bible books are called "books of wisdom." Both were written to show people how to live in a way that pleases God and to show that life without God has no meaning. Pleasure, success, being rich—none of these can make people happy for long. God is more important than all these things.

BE A WISE GUY

"Do this!" "Don't do that!" "Go to bed!" "Get up!" Does it seem like everyone is telling you what to do and how to do it? Do you sometimes tune out? Read Proverbs 2:1–15; 3:1–10 for some great advice from a real wise guy.

Think About It

- Being wise means being able to make good decisions. What's the difference between being smart and being wise? Can you be smart but not wise? Why or why not?
- One way to get wisdom is through experience. How else might you get wisdom? Why do you need it?
- Name some areas you could use wisdom in (like understanding school work or dealing with anger). How will being wise help you in those situations?
- Name ways you can use wisdom to help others.

Go Deeper

Read 1 Kings 3:4–15; Psalm 111:10; Proverbs 1:1–33; 3:11–35.

Prayer Starter

Think of two places in your life where you need wisdom. Maybe it's in dealing with family members and friends, or in thinking things through before you act. Ask God for the wisdom you need to deal with those situations.

Facts and Fun

Proverbs give advice on everyday life. They often have two parts—the good and the bad (see Proverbs 10:4). Mom's words sometimes sound like proverbs: "Walking in puddles will make wet shoes; staying on the path will keep them dry." Make up some proverbs of your own—they can be wise, wacky, or way-out. Have fun!

Coming Up Next:

Most people want to be the best, most important, or number one. But what's the best of the best? Find out . . . next time!

PAY ATTENTION!

Bells ring, sirens blare, fire alarms sound, and whistles blow to get our attention. It's usually a very good idea to pay attention to what's around you because it could mean the difference between danger and safety. Read Proverbs 4:1–23 to find another thing to pay attention to.

Think About It

- If God gave you a chance to choose anything in the world and said He would give it to you, what would you choose?
- Solomon says wisdom is the best thing anyone can have. God's wisdom is "supreme"—super, super good! How do you think God's wisdom is different from the wisdom of people?
- Think of some wise people in your life to whom you can go for good advice. How can they help you? What would you discuss with them or ask about? What makes them wise? How do you know their advice is good?
- Can you give good advice to someone? Why or why not?

Go Deeper

Read Proverbs 4:24–27; 6:1–23; 8:1–36; James 3:17.

Prayer Starter

Did you ever see or hear something that you had a hard time getting out of your mind? Some things stay with us a long time. That's why Proverbs 4:23 says to be careful what you think about. Ask God to help you be wise and think about things that are good.

Facts and Fun

What are ten things you can always count on? (*Answer: Your fingers.*)

Coming Up Next:

Boring and super-cool, straight A's and flunking out, millionaire and beggar. What do these have in common? (*Answer: They're opposites.*) Learn about opposites . . . next time!

ADVICE/THOUGHTS/WISDOM

A WORD (OR TWO) TO THE WISE

True or false, yes or no, this or that, either/or—all these phrases tell us that we must make a choice between two things. Read Proverbs 10:1–25 for a list of choices and their results.

Think About It

- Here's a simple science question. If you let a carton of milk sit on a picnic table on a hot summer day, what happens? Put the milk in the refrigerator and what happens? The answers are opposites and would probably cause you to make a choice on what to do with the milk.
- In science there is a reaction for every action. Each proverb lists opposite actions and the results of following those actions. Choose five proverbs in chapter 10. What is the main thing they say to do? What's the result?
- Many of these proverbs speak of a righteous person, someone who does what is good and pleases God. Think of three things you do that are good and pleasing to God. Now think of one thing you do that might need changing.

Go Deeper

Read Psalm 119:98–99; Proverbs 9:1–18; 11:1–31; 2 Timothy 3:15.

Prayer Starter

Make a proverb you read a prayer, asking God for help to be on the right side of it. For example: "God help me please my parents, and keep me from making them sad" (from verse 1).

Facts and Fun

If Solomon wrote five proverbs a day, how long would it take him to write 3,000? What if each one took three tries to get it right? That's a lot of writing!

Coming Up Next:

Walk the walk and talk the talk. Or is it walk the talk? Or is it walk, don't talk? Find out . . . next time!

CHOICES/GROWTH/RIGHTEOUSNESS

TALK THE TALK

Does your family or classroom have a list of rules or guidelines along with what happens when they are broken? Proverbs is a lot like that, except that it's really statements about how life works. Read Proverbs 14:1–23 for more life lessons.

Think About It

- What would your life be like if you did all the positive things mentioned in these proverbs? Think you could handle a life like that?
- The book of Proverbs is a guide to everyday living—what to say and do to get along with God and other people. Which of the proverbs you read can help guide you in your life?
- Many of these proverbs deal with what we say and how they affect people around us. What kind of words can help others? What words can hurt others? What do we need to remember in order to speak "wisely?"

Go Deeper

Read Exodus 20:20; Psalm 12:2–4; Proverbs 12:1–13:25.

Prayer Starter

Write some good things you say (when you're happy or someone is nice to you) and some not-so-good things you say (when you're angry or upset). Ask God to help you add to your "good" list and subtract from the "not-so-good" one.

Facts and Fun

Some "twisted" words:

Excitedly announcing the birth of his son, the father said, "The baby weighs 22 pounds and is 6 ½ inches long!"

A preacher told about the wonderful gifts brought to Jesus by the wise men: gold, Frankenstein, and myrrh.

Coming Up Next:

To be or not to be: astronaut; artist; car washer; grump. . . . Do you sometimes wonder who and what you should be to be happy? Learn what God wants you to be . . . next time!

THIS WAY TO HAPPINESS

It's important to watch road signs when you travel. They tell you which roads to take and when to turn to get where you want to go. Read Proverbs 15:1–24 for some road signs that'll help you steer clear of disaster!

Think About It

- Kindness, obedience, prayer, and being satisfied with what you have are some of the "road signs" that Christians follow in order to live as God wants them to. Can you think of others? Which of these are hardest for you to follow? Why?
- Solomon mentions cheerfulness several times in Proverbs 15. What do you think he means?
- How can taking control of your feelings and working to have a good attitude help you?
- Think of times when are you the happiest and most cheerful. What is your attitude at those times? Name three ways you can get a cheerful attitude (for example, you can think about good things in your life, get involved in something you really like, or help others).

Go Deeper

Read 2 Chronicles 10:7; Proverbs 16:1–17:20; Isaiah 30:21.

Prayer Starter

Having a good attitude helps you to be happy and cheerful. Ask God to help you have a good attitude and outlook on life.

Facts and Fun

Knock, knock! *Who's there?*
Howie. *Howie, who?*
Howie gonna have fun if you're not happy?

Coming Up Next:

Did you ever make great plans and then have them completely fall apart—and it's not your fault? Or maybe it was a wee bit your fault? Find out the other side of the story . . . next time!

IT'S NOT MY FAULT!

Have you ever planned something and had everything go wrong? Were you **SO** mad—because it wasn't your fault that things fell apart? Read Proverbs 19:1–23 for another side of the story.

Think About It

- Emergencies, illness, and lots of other things we can't control can make things go wrong. How do your attitude and feelings affect how things turn out?
- What do you do, who do you blame, when things don't go the way you planned? Why?
- When you're making plans or choices, what influences you to do it a certain way—friends, parents, what's popular? How might some of your plans and choices change if you choose to follow God's way?

Go Deeper

Read Joshua 24:15; Ruth 1:15–16; Proverbs 18:1–24; 20:1–30.

Prayer Starter

Choose two or three short verses from Proverbs 19:1–23 and use them as a prayer today. Some good verses to use are 8, 20, or 23.

Facts and Fun

A doctor's proverb:

Take strong medicine and a cold will go away in a week; but if you do nothing, the cold will last for seven days.

Coming Up Next:

How can you become a superperson in a few months (besides miraculously becoming a superhero)? Find out the training secret . . . next time!

PERSONAL TRAINER

If a trainer could turn you into an incredible athlete in six months, would you follow his directions? Read Proverbs 22:1–25 to find out what God's training can do for you!

Think About It

- Describe what a spiritual and godly "superperson" would be like. How would he or she act, talk, and so on?
- Could you become that superperson? Why or why not?
- Who "trains" you in the way you should go? According to what you read today, what's included in God's training plan? How can you follow it?
- Think of things you've learned since you were born—walking, talking, reading. You will use these your whole life. How can learning about God when you're young help you the rest of your life (for example, it can keep you from making serious mistakes you'll regret later)?

Go Deeper

Read Proverbs 21:1–31; 23:1–35; Matthew 7:16–20; Galatians 5:22–23.

Prayer Starter

One of the exercises needed to be a "super" follower of God is daily prayer. After praying for your family and friends, ask God to be your personal trainer.

Facts and Fun

What did one math teacher say to another? *(Answer: I've got a problem.)*

Why did Jake go to night school? *(Answer: So he could learn to read in the dark.)*

What do a teacher and an eye doctor have in common? *(Answer: They both stare at pupils.)*

Coming Up Next:

What do you think is the mightiest muscle in your body? You may be surprised! Find out . . . next time!

THE MIGHTIEST MUSCLE

If someone says, "Show me your muscle," what do you do? Probably make a fist and bend your arm to make your bicep pop up. But if you want to show your mightiest muscle, you should stick out your tongue! Read Proverbs 25:1–25 to find out why.

Think About It
- What things does this small muscle rule?
- Solomon uses words like "argue," "boast," and "quarrelsome" to describe some bad acts of the tongue. Of course, the tongue only says what the person is thinking. What do you really need to keep under control?
- What motivates us to say bad things or have bad thoughts (for example, jealousy, anger)? Are the thoughts and words that come out of your mouth good to hear? Do these things please God?

Go Deeper
Read Proverbs 24:1–34; 26:1–28; James 3:1–12.

Prayer Starter
Think of your tongue and what it says. Does it spout out bad language and words that hurt people, or kind and helpful words? Ask God to help you have an attitude that causes you to think and say things that are good and kind and please Him.

Facts and Fun
"Apples of gold" in Proverbs 25:11 that you read seems to be talking about some kind of decoration or centerpiece on a table. Or it may refer to a carving done in gold over silver. Either way, it is pointing out something that is very beautiful and valuable. Our speech should be like those apples of gold.

Coming Up Next:
Does "What you see is what you get" describe you? Would you like to change some things that people "see" in you? Read some suggestions for a makeover . . . next time!

THE REAL ME

Some people put on fancy clothes and say, "This is the real me." Others wear beat-up clothes and say, "This is the real me." Neither name brand clothes nor cool hairstyles show the real you. Read Proverbs 27:1–24 for the REAL answer.

Think About It
• What do you do to look cool? What can you do to be truly cool . . . on the inside?
• Name five things in your heart (for example, peace, jealousy, wanting to be liked, etc.). How do they make up your personality—who you are? Why is having things in your heart that are pleasing to God important? How could that change you and what you do?

Go Deeper
Read Psalm 19:14; Proverbs 28:1–29:27; Matthew 5:8.

Prayer Starter
Write ten words that describe who you are (like chatty, kind, or grumpy)—be honest. Ask God to help you improve and develop the good things and weaken or get rid of the bad ones.

Facts and Fun
Job descriptions:
Archaeologist: a scientist whose life is in ruins.
Frozen police officer: a copsicle.
Short-order cook: a person who prepares food for children.
Stagecoach: a theatrical instructor

Coming Up Next:
What things amaze or puzzle you? What great mysteries would you love to solve? Discover some new ones . . . next time!

PUZZLING WORDS!

Eureka! Hooray! All right! I did it! Those are really fun words to blare out at the top of your voice because they mean you've made a discovery or solved a problem. Read Proverbs 30:5–31 to find some amazing, eye-opening puzzles and words!

Think About It

- Agur asks God for two things. What would you ask God for? Why?
- What about God and His world amaze you? What is the most amazing of all?
- Agur lists creatures that are small but wise. What can you learn about God from small things such as ants, birds, and small children?

Go Deeper

Read Proverbs 31:1–31; Matthew 5:18–19; 1 Thessalonians 2:13.

Prayer Starter

Think of three or four things about God or the Bible that puzzle you and ask God to help you understand them. Thank God for some of the amazing things He's made.

Facts and Fun

Maybe Solomon ran out of wise sayings or maybe he was having a "no brainer" week. Or maybe Agur got the point across in a more amusing manner. Whatever! Agur wrote chapter 30. Nothing is known about him except that he was a wise teacher. He may not have been a Jew but a non-Israelite who chose to worship the one true God. Of course, other nations had wise guys, too!

Coming Up Next:

Do you have lots of things to do and not enough time to do even half of them? Learn about time . . . next time!

WHAT TIME IS IT?

Any clocks in your house? How about calendars and schedules? Any sundials or hourglasses? Seriously, there are lots of ways to know what it's time to do. Read Ecclesiastes 3:1–17 to find out.

Think About It
- Tick, tick, tick. Time is running out! That can be tense if your team is one point ahead in a basketball game with 10 seconds left. It can be exciting if it's the last hour before summer vacation. How is time important in your life?
- There are times when things go wrong, but many times good things balance them out. What would you do about good and bad times if you were in control of the way things happen in your life?
- Which of the "times" in the chapter are you in right now? How can you enjoy it? Or make it through?

Go Deeper
Read Ecclesiastes 1:1–2:26; Romans 11:33–36; 1 Peter 1:3–6.

Prayer Starter
How much time do you spend doing activities on a weekday—school, playing, sleeping, praying, and other things? Thank God for one thing you really like about each of those times.

Facts and Fun
Clocks have been around for a very long time. One of the first was a sundial that used shadows to tell the time. They've also been made from water and sand!

Coming Up Next:
Ever say, "I'm just a kid—what can I do?" Well, you'd be surprised! Investigate some exciting possibilities . . . next time!

YOU'RE ONLY YOUNG ONCE

Adventurous! Generous! How are the two connected? The writer of Ecclesiastes 11:1–12:7 tells you to be both and to enjoy life. He also warns you not to fool around with "what ifs" and "maybes." To find some special advice for young people, read what he says.

Think About It
- Imagine you could be who you wanted a year from now. What kind of person would you be? What are your hopes for next month? For next year? According to Ecclesiastes, how can you ensure the best future for yourself?
- In Ecclesiastes 12:2–7 the Teacher talks about growing old and all the troubles that can come with old age. How do you feel about old people? How do you feel about getting old yourself? How does it help to know that God is always with you—when you're young and until you die?

Go Deeper
Read Proverbs 22:6; Ecclesiastes 5:1–20; 7:1–22; 2 Timothy 3:15.

Prayer Starter
Think of ten things that you can do because you are young. Thank God for these great "young" things and for ways to enjoy them.

Facts and Fun
A kid was saying the books of the Old Testament, "Job, Psalms, Proverbs . . . Enthusiastics."

Coming Up Next:
How do you feel about love songs? Yuck? Or sigh? Read the best love song ever . . . next time!

FOLLOWING GOD

SONG OF SONGS

Most of the hit songs these days are love songs. Love has always been a popular theme for songs. Well, here is the love song of all love songs. Now, don't giggle when you hear the word "love." Everyone needs love in his or her life. Babies don't thrive and may even die if they don't get it. We feel cranky and grouchy when we think no one loves us.

God knows all about what we feel and need. In the Song of Songs, God shows us that the love we have for each other is a beautiful part of His plan for our lives. This book tells of the love between a man and a woman and points out how wonderful love and commitment can be. The Song of Songs also shows God's love for His people.

The phrase "Song of Songs" means the greatest or best of songs.

Who is this lovebird?

Most people think King Solomon wrote the Song of Songs, and it is sometimes called the Song of Solomon. Some people think an unknown writer wrote it and set it to music. It could also have been many poems written by several writers, including Solomon, that were later gathered together.

The Song of Songs may have been written while Solomon was king or just after his reign.

It's quite the love story!

This book is a poem about the love between a man and a woman. Their love story gives a wonderful picture of God's love for His people, a love that is special, giving, and forgiving. God wants us to love each other and be happy. We also know that God loves us even more than anyone else loves us! Now that really is worth singing about!

LOVING WORDS

How do you feel about reading love poems? Do you really enjoy them or do they make you want to hide under the table? Read Song of Songs 1:1–11; 2:1–4 to take in a biblical love poem.

Think About It
- Do you think a love poem belongs in the Bible? Why or why not?
- If someone was going to describe you lovingly as an animal or plant, what would you like to be? Why?
- If the wisest man who ever lived valued love so highly, what does that tell you about love? How is the love described like God's love for you?

Go Deeper
Read Song of Songs 2:5–4:16; John 13:34; Romans 5:8.

Prayer Starter
Think of people you love and those who love you—family, friends, uncles and aunts, grandparents, and any others that come to mind. Thank God for His love and the love of others.

Facts and Fun
Doves and lilies:
Doves were considered clean and calm. Someone with the "eyes of a dove" had a beautiful calm character.

Lilies were common flowers and the woman was saying she wasn't so special. But Solomon said she was as special as a lily among thorns.

Coming Up Next:
How would you describe the person you loved best of all? How would you like someone to describe you? Discover how the king described his love . . . next time!

A BRIDE LIKE A GOAT!

Have you ever been to a wedding? Everyone waits expectantly for the star to appear—the bride. Then the people "ooh and aah" over her and say how beautiful she is. Read Song of Songs 6:1–12; 8:5–7; Revelation 19:6–10 to learn about the perfect bride.

Think About It
- The king uses many things to describe the woman he loves—cities, troops, goats, sheep, fruit, and a dove. Which of these is your best friend like? Why?
- Revelation tells about the wedding of the Lamb (Jesus) and the perfect bride (all Christians.) What do you think that wedding might be like (awesome? quiet? huge bands?)?
- Christ's love for the church and for you is better than the love of anyone else because He died for you and now you can live together forever. How can Christ's love affect the way you feel toward others?

Go Deeper
Read Song of Songs 5:1–16; 7:1–13; Ephesians 5:25–32; Revelation 21:2, 9.

Prayer Starter
Write a love poem to God. Tell Him all the things you love about Him—for example, His care, His power, His forgiveness.

Facts and Fun
Circle every third letter below to discover what Jesus says about love.

BRAMPSLZITUHONAQPVRWEAGLIMOYRVXPESMDTEYXC
OHJUBXSEROPMYWQOBXUYEMPJUEESKLTJSLPQOMZVR
SEPKOHGNDSEZFAYWNPLOGFTBCHWMEASR. (John 13:34)

Coming Up Next:
Ever been just bursting with a really important announcement but no one wanted to listen to you? Learn about a man whose message was totally ignored . . . next time!

W hat do God on His throne, angels with six wings, burning coals, and time moving backward have in common? They are all found in the book of Isaiah. Isaiah also tells about Jesus' birth, suffering, and death which did not happen until seven hundred years later! Come along with Isaiah to learn of God's judgment and forgiveness.

A prophet was someone who spoke for God, telling the people and their leaders about God's commands and promises. Because they told the people to obey God and quit their evil ways, they were not very popular. But, even though no one usually paid much attention to their messages, the prophets kept on telling the truth about God.

The book of Isaiah is the first of the writings of the prophets in the Bible. Isaiah had the longest ministry of any of them. He prophesied for 60 years through the best and worst times of Israel. That's probably about six times as long as you have lived!

Isaiah was a prophet to four kings of Judah, but he preaches to the whole nation of Israel as well, telling them to quit doing evil and turn back to God. He warns the people to shape up and love God with all their hearts and minds. He hopes they would see how wicked and disobedient they are and change their ways.

Where did Isaiah get all this stuff?

The prophet Isaiah, son of Amoz, wrote the book of Isaiah. Every word in the book is what God told him to write. The events in the first half of the book happened during the middle of Isaiah's time of preaching, so they were probably written about 700 B.C. But chapters 40–66 were likely written near the end of Isaiah's life, about 681 B.C.

Oh, behave!

Isaiah was written to tell the people of Judah that God will punish them if they keep disobeying Him. The first half tells of God's anger over their sin and His coming judgment. But the second half tells of God's love and forgiveness. It explains how God wants to take His people back and comfort them.

Isaiah also tells Judah that the Messiah is coming. He will save them, and God's people will be made perfect through Him (Jesus).

MESSIAH MESSAGES

Many people claim they can predict the future. They claim to have ESP, magic cards, or visions. Most of their claims are just crazy! But read Isaiah 7:13–14; 9:6–7; 42:1–4; 52:13–53:12 for a REAL prediction.

Think About It
- These prophecies about the Messiah, Jesus, really came true hundreds of years later. They were written and were part of the Jewish Bible *long before* any of the New Testament took place or was written. What does that tell you about God and His Word?
- Why do you think Isaiah told the Israelites about the future? Why did it matter to them?
- The Bible is one big story telling us about sin, God's love, and Jesus as our Savior. God's words always come true. What are two ways that knowing that the Bible is true can help you want to live as a follower of God?

Go Deeper
Read Isaiah 11:1–10; 50:5–7; 61:1–3; Luke 2:10–12; John 19:28–30.

Prayer Starter
Read Luke 1:31; 18:31–33 and think of how Isaiah's prophecies about Jesus came true. Amazing! Tell God how you feel about the fact that He is always truthful and that He knows the future.

Facts and Fun
In Isaiah's day few people cared about God. They prayed to idols and some even sacrificed their children. It wasn't a good time or place to be a kid! Isaiah's words could have saved the people but they didn't believe what he said.

Coming Up Next:
Where can you see six-winged angels, burning coals, and a shaking building? No, it's not a movie. Find out . . . next time!

AN AWESOME MEETING

What would you do if you were going to meet the most important person in your whole country? Read Isaiah 6:1–13; 9:8–13; 10:5–6, 12, 24–25 to find out about such a meeting and what happened afterward.

Think About It

• Put yourself in Isaiah's place when he saw God in the temple. What would it have been like? How do you think you would have reacted? Why? What might you learn about God from such a meeting?

• God wanted Isaiah to take an important message to the people of Judah. It was a message of warnings but it also showed God's love. Why did the people need to hear both parts of this message?

• What do you think God wants you to tell others about Him? Who can you tell?

Go Deeper

Read Ezekiel 18:25–32; Daniel 4:34–37; Revelation 4:1–11.

Prayer Starter

Every time you pray you have a meeting with God. Discuss two or three important things in your life with Him. Then pray for three people you know who don't know God.

Facts and Fun

There are thousands and maybe millions of angels. In Matthew 26:53, Jesus talks about "more than 12 legions of angels" (a Roman legion had 6,000 soldiers.) The angels Isaiah saw surrounding God were the seraphim (SAIR-uh-fim). This is the highest rank of angels, who serve in God's presence. A seraph has three pairs of wings.

Coming Up Next:

Do you turn cartwheels, yell, or jump around when something wonderful happens? Learn how someone responded . . . next time!

MORE SOLID THAN ROCK!

After lots of doom and gloom, there seems to be a sudden upturn in Isaiah's messages. Read Isaiah 26:1–21 for a welcome break.

Think About It

- What is the strongest, most solid thing you know? How is God like that thing?
- The Old Testament often describes God and His love as a rock. What does that mean to you? What does it tell you about how trustworthy He is?
- Isaiah worshiped and praised God for who He was and what He did. What can you worship God for? Why would you want to?

Go Deeper

Read Psalm 18:1–3; 92:12–15; Isaiah 25:1–12; 27:1–13.

Prayer Starter

Read Luke 1:68–75 as a prayer today. This song was sung by Zechariah hundreds of years after Isaiah lived and just before Jesus was born. Praise God for how solid He is. Ask for faith to lean on Him.

Facts and Fun

Knock, knock! *Who's there?*
Isaiah. *Isaiah, who?*
I say "ah" when I go to the doctor.

Coming Up Next:

Have you ever read a story, cartoon, or joke and laughed so hard you cried or fell down laughing? Learn about what brings true joy . . . next time!

DYING OF THIRST

Imagine that you haven't had water for days; the land is dry and sandy. Suddenly you come over a hill and—wow! Read Isaiah 35:1–10; 40:1–11 to learn more about this and other wonders.

Think About It
- What would the sudden blooming in a desert be like? If you were in that desert, how would you react?
- Why do you think Isaiah used this picture? Can you think of other pictures that would be as great?
- Isaiah tells of the joy, freedom, healing, and hope we have with God. How does God's joy show up in your life (for example, in a friend's hug, giggling for no reason . . .)?

Go Deeper
Read Psalm 4:6–8; Isaiah 41:8–20; 43:1–13; Romans 15:12–13.

Prayer Starter
Think of how God has blessed you and helped you when you were in a "desert" place—helping you in a new school, healing you when you were very sick, or giving you friends when you were lonely. Thank Him for how He helped you.

Facts and Fun
"A voice of one calling . . . a voice says" (Isaiah 40:3, 6)

People who heard Isaiah thought he was talking about the return of the Jews from Babylon. We know from the New Testament that this was also a prophecy about John the Baptist (Matthew 3:3). John announced the coming of Jesus and baptized Him when He came.

Coming Up Next:
Do you know someone who is always bragging? Listen to a really big braggart and the whopping lesson he never forgot . . . next time!

KING OF THE HILL!

Imagine the yelling, stamping enemy army that had conquered every major city in Judah is now camped at the gate of your city. Your survival and the honor of Hezekiah, king of Judah, is on the line. Read Isaiah 36:1–3, 13–20; 37:1–7, 36–37 for the story.

Think About It

- If you had been trapped in Jerusalem with the Jews, how would you have felt? What would you have done? How would you have responded to Isaiah? Why?
- What "armies" seem to have you trapped (for example, loneliness, fear . . .)?
- How can you become like Hezekiah when you face trouble? If God doesn't answer your prayer right away, what can you do?

Go Deeper

Read 2 Kings 6:24–25; 7:1–20; Matthew 7:7–11; 1 Thessalonians 5:16–17.

Prayer Starter

Print PRAYER along the side of a paper. Write one or more things to pray about beside each letter. (P=peace, patience, people, etc.) Add the "armies" you face. Then pray for them.

Facts and Fun

Where did Hezekiah keep his armies? *(Answer: In his sleevies!)*

Coming Up Next:

What's the weight of the earth or the number of the stars? Just exactly how many grains of dust are on earth? Who knows? Find out . . . next time!

PRAYER

YOU MEAN YOU DON'T KNOW?

Have you ever gotten into a conversation where you didn't have a clue what the other person was talking about? When you ask, "What are you talking about?" she might say, "You mean you don't know?" Of course, she will probably tell you what you need to know. Read Isaiah 40:12–31; 51:12–16 to discover how God makes it clear what He wants us to know.

Think About It
- Try to picture the most incredible, dazzling, beautiful thing in the world. How is God like and unlike that thing?
- What do you think is the most awesome thing about God? Why?
- What is God telling you about Himself in these verses? God is the incredibly powerful King of the universe. In what ways is that important to you (for example, He can heal you if you're sick, help you understand science . . .)?

Go Deeper
Read Psalm 95:1–7; Isaiah 45:1–25; Ephesians 3:20.

Prayer Starter
Could you run two miles and not get tired? If you were an eagle, you could easily go two miles gliding along on warm air currents. God's strength is like a current of warm air carrying us along through troubles and tough times. Thank Him for being King of the universe. Tell Him where you need His help.

Facts and Fun
"Circle of the earth" (Isaiah 40:22)

Many people in olden times thought the world was flat and probably square so you could fall off it if you went far enough! But this verse seems to show that Isaiah knew the world was round!

Coming Up Next:
What do you do with a piece of wood or a stone? How about praying to them? Not! But meet some people who thought that was a good idea . . . next time!

THE CREATOR/GOD

YOU GOTTA BE KIDDING!

Got a problem? Pray to a piece of wood! Say what? That's how confused some of the Israelites were! God was constantly on their case about praying to idols. He even used humor to get His point across. Read Isaiah 44:9–20; 46:1–10 and smile.

Think About It

- Imagine making a LEGO® man and then trusting him to help you! God was showing the people how foolish it was to pray to idols. What other point do you think God was making?

- Idols aren't always statues. Anything that is more important to someone than God is an idol. Fun, money, "lots of stuff," popularity, importance, and fame could become "idols." Do you have any "idols" in your life that could become more important than God? What are they? Name five things you can do to "tear down" these idols (for example, give some money away, spend time with God instead of a video game).

Go Deeper

Read Isaiah 41:1–7, 21–29; Habakkuk 2:18–20; 1 Corinthians 8:4–6.

Prayer Starter

Think of some things that might be too important to you, such as being popular or having all the latest and coolest things. Talk to God about them. Ask for help to always make God most important. Praise Him for being the only true God.

Facts and Fun

Knock, knock! *Who's there?*
Wood. *Wood, who?*
Wood you like to come out and pray to me?

Coming Up Next:

When you're on the bottom, so low you have to look up to see a worm, the only way you can go is up. Climb upward . . . next time!

WANT TO BE A TATTOO?

Ever been told, "I'm counting to ten! You better shape up now!"? God had been telling the Jews to "shape up" for many, many years. Finally, Jerusalem was destroyed and the people were carried off. But that wasn't the end. Read Isaiah 49:8–26; 52:1–3 for the rest of the story.

Think About It
- God loved the Jews and forgave them. What would it have been like to know God still loved them? How does knowing God loves you that way affect how you live?
- Think of a time when you did a serious wrong and received a serious punishment. If you had known you would get treats after the punishment, how would it have been different? What would it have told you about how your parents felt?

Go Deeper
Read Isaiah 51:4–12; Romans 11:6; Ephesians 2:5–7.

Prayer Starter
As you pray, hold your hands in front of you, palms up. Write "God" on them with washable markers to remind you of His love. Think of how God always remembers you—just as if you were tattooed on His hands. Thank Him for that.

Facts and Fun
"Engraved you on the palms of my hands" (Isaiah 49:16)
    The Israelites were forbidden to tattoo their bodies (Leviticus 19:28) but tattooing was common among the pagans in the ancient Middle East. The Israelites knew that people would tattoo the name of someone they loved on their bodies. So God used this expression to help them understand that He was always concerned about them.

Coming Up Next:
Secret plans are exciting. Especially if you're in the loop! Read about a really incredible, wonderful plan . . . next time!

WOW! WHAT A PLAN!

Wars, enemy armies, killings, and being taken captive were all part of Isaiah's message. Today Isaiah might be called Dr. Doom. But that wasn't all! God also offered hope! Read Isaiah 54:10–55:13 to learn of God's plans for the Jews.

Think About It

- If you had been a kid in Jerusalem in Isaiah's time, how do you think you would have reacted to his messages of doom? How about his message of hope?
- God says His thoughts and ways are different from ours. What are some ways God thinks and acts differently than you (for example, He knows all things, He is always fair, loving, and forgiving)? Why is that a good thing?
- God had good plans for the Jews. And He has plans for you. What do you think some of God's plan for you might include (for example, become a good musician or scientist, understand the Bible)?

Go Deeper

Read Isaiah 54:1–9; Ephesians 1:11; Hebrews 11:40.

Prayer Starter

Think of some plans you might have for now and for when you grow up. Tell God about your plans and ask for help to discover what *His* plans are for you.

Facts and Fun

Student to teacher: I plan to be a famous mountaineer and climb the highest mountain.

   Teacher to student: Better plan on doing your homework then or you won't even be able to climb to the next grade!

Coming Up Next:

Hungry, homeless, hurting people are all around us. What can you do to help? Anything? Find out . . . next time!

TURN ON THE LIGHT!

You're trying to read but it's dark in the room. Mom says, "Turn on the light." What an improvement! Read Isaiah 57:14–21; 58:6–12 to find out about how to be the light.

Think About It

- We can see what's important to God in these verses. How does He feel about those who love Him? How does God feel about the needy?
- Choose a name for yourself like "Repairer of Broken Friendships" or "Giver of Gifts." How can you make that name be true for you?
- What other ways can you help others who are in need, such as the homeless, sick, or lonely? How might your help change their lives?

Go Deeper

Read Isaiah 59:1–21; Matthew 25:34–40; James 1:27.

Prayer Starter

Go to a dark place for prayer today like a closet or window-less room. As you sit in the darkness, think of the different needs people have. Then turn on the light and think of God's help. Ask God for ways you can be His light to others.

Facts and Fun

"Your light will rise in the darkness" (Isaiah 58:10).

What would you do without electricity? In Isaiah's day, darkness stopped most activities and brought all sorts of threats and dangers. So darkness became a symbol for evil and light represented goodness. Here light stands for the people's acts of kindness and mercy.

Coming Up Next:

Nobody can predict what will happen, except . . . well, you'll find out . . . next time!

HELPING OTHERS

A FANTASTIC FUTURE

Imagine being severely injured and needing to relearn to walk. You want to give up but the therapist never gives up. He knows, with hard work, the future will be much better. Read Isaiah 60:1–22 for plans of an awesome future.

Think About It

- If God could "order" the perfect place for you, what would it be like? How is it like or unlike the place God describes here?
- God describes how wonderful Zion will be and how His light will protect it. Read Revelation 21:23 to find out how this applies to God's people in heaven.
- God knows your future too—even your future after you die. He has great things in store for you. How does knowing that affect you now? What can you do to make sure you get God's fantastic future?

Go Deeper

Read Isaiah 61:1–62:12; John 14:1–4; Revelation 7:16–17.

Prayer Starter

A song starts like this: "Heaven is a wonderful place, full of . . ." Finish the song with your own words that tell what you think heaven will be full of. Thank God that heaven is in your future if you belong to Jesus.

Facts and Fun

Knock, knock! *Who's there?*
Zion. *Zion, who?*
Zion time, or has the party already started?

Coming Up Next:

Ever tear a project apart and then do it all over a much better way? Be part of an amazing redo . . . next time!

OUT WITH THE OLD, IN WITH THE NEW

Has your family ever remodeled where you live? When the work is done, everything looks totally different. Read Isaiah 63:7–16; 65:17–25 to learn about God's amazing "redo."

Think About It
- God's patience with the Israelites tells us how He'll be with us. Why do you think He was so good to them? To you?
- In Isaiah 65:17–25 Isaiah describes a place that is eternal, safe, peaceful, and with plenty of everything for everyone. If there was such a place right next door, what kinds of things would you do to get in? Why?
- You can get into such a place! Believe in Jesus as your Savior. That doesn't mean you can sin and do anything you please, though. What does it mean to you?

Go Deeper
Read Psalm 16:11; Isaiah 64:1–12; John 14:1–4.

Prayer Starter
Think of God's patience with you, even when you blow it. Think about why He's like that and thank Him for it.

Facts and Fun
Imagine a new heaven and a new earth with different rules: maybe you could fly or breathe under water. What would you change in the new earth? What do you think God will change?

Coming Up Next:
Idols and idolatry everywhere in Judah—what a mess! Meet someone God called when he was still a kid to help fix the mess . . . next time.

JEREMIAH & LAMENTATIONS

Are you ready to read Jeremiah? Are you sure? Wandering in the desert, being in prison, being thrown into a muddy well, and digging up buried pots are all a part of the prophet Jeremiah's life.

Jeremiah tells many people about their sins: kings, false prophets, people at the temple, and people at the gates of Jerusalem. Unfortunately, very few pay attention to what he says. They don't want to hear about God's judgment, and they often make life miserable for the poor prophet. But Jeremiah sees his prophecies fulfilled when enemy armies destroy Jerusalem and many of his people are taken captive.

In the book of Lamentations, Jeremiah writes about pain and suffering. Jerusalem is totally destroyed and empty and the people are far away in Babylon. Lamentations is both a sad and a hopeful book.

Okay, Baruch, write this down . . .

Jeremiah, who is a priest and prophet, receives the messages in both of these books from God. But Jeremiah's helper, Baruch, actually wrote down the prophecies as Jeremiah spoke them. So most of the book of Jeremiah was written while Jeremiah was still preaching (626–585 B.C.). The last verses were added later since we're told that Jeremiah's words end in chapter 51. They might have been added about 25 years after Jerusalem was destroyed. Lamentations was written soon after Jerusalem's destruction when the horrible event was still fresh in Jeremiah's mind.

Listen up, people!

These books were written to warn God's people to turn away from their sinful lives and come back to God. They also show that God suffers when His people suffer.

Jeremiah is faithful to God even when the people don't listen to him and make fun of him. He tells the people of God's judgment. But Jeremiah knows that God is faithful. He will not let His people suffer forever. Jeremiah tells them that God will forgive them and bring them back to their own land in 70 years. And God keeps His promises.

LOOKING FOR ONE HONEST AND TRUTHFUL PERSON

In basketball, you're out of the game after five fouls. In baseball you sit on the bench after three strikes. Were the people of Judah zapped out of existence after three or five warnings? Nope! God kept sending prophet after prophet to warn them to change their sinful ways. Read Jeremiah 1:4–10; 5:1–15 to meet one of His prophets and hear his warning.

Think About It
- If you were Jeremiah, how would you have reacted to God's words about His plan for you? Why?
- How did God convince Jeremiah that He would help him? Why do you think it was important for Jeremiah to know God would be with him?
- What are some things you can you do to become the kind of person God was looking for? Will that be easy for you? Why or why not?

Go Deeper
Read Jeremiah 2:11–19, 27–35; Matthew 22:34–39; Luke 11:28.

Prayer Starter
Read Psalm 119:1–8 as a prayer today.

Facts and Fun
What one thing in life can you never count on? *(Answer: The past minute.)*

Coming Up Next:
Grab a box of tissues and get ready for a sad, sad state of affairs. A real heartbreaker. Learn about someone who feels like crying his eyeballs out . . . next time!

FOUNTAIN EYES!

Did you ever feel so sad about something that all you could do is cry? Read Jeremiah 9:1–6; 13:15–17; Lamentations 3:39–51 to find out what made Jeremiah weep.

Think About It
- Think about the world all around you. Killing, unfaithfulness, and lying were some of the things that made Jeremiah cry. How many of these do you see around you? How do you feel about them? Why?
- If the people's sin made Jeremiah sad, what do you think would have gotten him jumping for joy? What changes in your world would get you jumping for joy?
- How do you think God feels when He looks at your life—sad, happy, hopeful? Why? Think of what things you may need to change to make God happy.

Go Deeper
Read 1 Chronicles 28:9; Psalm 40:16; Jeremiah 9:7–19; Lamentations 3:52–64.

Prayer Starter
Think of the game of Hide-and-Seek. Are you trying to hide something from God? Or are you seeking Him and what He wants you to do? Talk to God about it. Ask for help to want to live His way.

Facts and Fun
Knock, knock! *Who's there?*
Boo. *Boo, who?*
Why are you crying?

Coming Up Next:
How are people like a spinning, slimy, wet pot? Find out . . . next time!

A HUNK OF CLAY

Ever made things from clay? How do your creations turn out—as beautiful vases or lopsided dishes? The nice thing about clay is that if you don't like your creation you can mush it together and start over. Read Jeremiah 18:1–12; Isaiah 64:8 to learn about God's hunk of clay.

Think About It

- If you were about to create something from clay, how would you decide what to make?
- God used a common job in Judah, the job of a potter, to get His message across. Isaiah says God is the potter and you are the clay. How might God decide what to make people into?
- Imagine yourself as a hunk of clay in God's hands. What do or don't you like about that idea? What kind of thing or person would you want God to make you into? Why?

Go Deeper

Read Jeremiah 19:1–20:6; Romans 9:16–23; 2 Timothy 2:20–21.

Prayer Starter

Take a chunk of clay or play dough and squish it around in your hands as you pray. Ask God to shape you into the person He wants you to be.

Facts and Fun

The Sunday school teacher told the class how God formed the first man from the dust of the earth. Kyle thought about that and then said, "If Adam was made out of the dust of the earth, why doesn't he turn to mud when he takes a bath?"

Coming Up Next:

Just exactly how much trouble can you get into by telling the truth? Find out . . . next time!

LET'S SHUT HIM UP— PERMANENTLY!

Many of the people of Jerusalem were already getting tired of Jeremiah's preaching. But speaking in the courtyard of the temple really set them off! Read Jeremiah 26:1–24 to find out how Jeremiah's speech went over.

Think About It

- If God gave you a message like this for your country and told you to go tell everyone at your church, how would you feel? What would you need to help you obey?
- God told Jeremiah to tell the people His entire message— not to leave out a single word. Why was this important? What parts might Jeremiah have been tempted to leave out? What parts of God's message might you be tempted to leave out? Why?
- What made Jeremiah so brave? How can you be brave like him?

Go Deeper

Read Job 13:15; Psalm 27:1; Jeremiah 36:1–32.

Prayer Starter

Think of three people you know who don't know about Jesus. Pray for each of them by name and ask God to help you share your faith with them.

Facts and Fun

When a boy was looking through the family Bible, a leaf that had been pressed between the pages fell out. The boy ran to his mother and said excitedly, "I think I just found Adam's suit!"

Coming Up Next:

From gloom and doom and more doom to blessings and hope and happiness. How do these all fit together? Find out . . . next time!

BAD NEWS, GOOD NEWS

Has anyone ever said to you, "I have some bad news and some good news?" Which one did you choose to hear first? Read Jeremiah 30:1–24 for God's "bad news, good news" for the people of Judah.

Think About It

- Jeremiah let the people of Judah have the bad news first. If Jeremiah were talking to you, what bad news might he tell you? What would you do about it?
- Jeremiah also had good news—the love and blessing of God. The people of Judah had been rotten for years. Why would God be so kind to them and promise them good things?
- What are some of the good things God promises you (for example, love, friends, contentment)? How do you react to these promises?

Go Deeper

Read Exodus 34:6–7; Psalm 145:9; Jeremiah 31:1–40.

Prayer Starter

Think of some "bad news" in your life, like bad grades, your best friend moves away, or your grandma is very sick. Then think of God's good news that He loves you and cares for you and your friends and family. Thank Him for it.

Facts and Fun

The "bad news" about being a good sport is that often you have to lose to prove it.

Coming Up Next:

"Okay boys, I know you don't like me, but this is getting out of hand! Don't throw me in! Don't . . . YAGHHH!" What's happening? Find out . . . next time!

HELLO DOWN THERE!

Imagine saying something in school and being sent to the principal's office, and then being given in-school detention for a week. What a bummer! Now imagine all that happened just because you delivered a message. Read Jeremiah 37:1–16; 38:4–13 to see how King Zedekiah reacted to Jeremiah's message.

Think About It

- Imagine you're King Zed. What would you hope Jeremiah could tell you?
- Jeremiah could have given the king a favorable report, but instead he said what God told him to say. Was it worth it? What do you think Jeremiah gained from obeying God?
- How do you react when someone wants you to do something wrong? Is it hard or easy for you to follow God when others are doing wrong things? Why? What good things do you gain (like trust) by following God?

Go Deeper

Read Psalm 40:8; Jeremiah 38:14–28; Philippians 2:13.

Prayer Starter

Read Psalm 1:1–6 as a prayer today.

Facts and Fun

A cistern was a large hole in the ground shaped like a bell with the narrow end at the top. The cistern was lined with rocks to collect rainwater. The bottom would have been dark, damp, and in this case, full of mud. A person could drown, die of exposure, or starve to death in a cistern.

Coming Up Next:

Jeremiah had warned the people of God's judgment so often that he sounded like a broken record. But suddenly the volume turned up. Read about it . . . next time!

I TOLD YOU SO!

You've heard the same thing for 40 years and it hasn't happened yet. But look out! Time's up! Read Jeremiah 39:1–40:6 for the end of the story.

Think About It
- Just because God waits patiently for us to be sorry for doing wrong things and change our ways doesn't mean He won't judge us. What did God finally do after all His warnings?
- Jeremiah had every right in the world to shake his finger at the king and the people of Judah and say, "I told you so!" when his prophecies were fulfilled. If you'd been there, what would you have thought when everything God said came true?
- How did God show Jeremiah that He is trustworthy and loving? Name five ways God shows His love to you. Think of three things that you trust God for.

Go Deeper
Read 2 Samuel 7:28; Jeremiah 42:1–43:7; John 17:15–17.

Prayer Starter
People don't always keep their word. You may break your promises sometimes too. But God is always trustworthy and keeps His word. Thank Him for doing that in your life.

Facts and Fun
A siege was a military blockade of a city to force it to surrender—no one could go in or out. Sieges often lasted until the food supply ran out and people began to suffer from starvation and disease. The Babylonian army laid siege to the city of Jerusalem for 18 months. The city of Ashdod once withstood a siege by the Egyptians for 29 years—the longest siege ever!

Coming Up Next:
Nobody believed him! All his life people laughed at Jeremiah. Find out how come they suddenly stopped laughing . . . next time!

JUSTICE WINS OUT

Jackals are kings in the city! Jerusalem lay in ruins and most of the people had been taken in chains to the faraway land of Babylon. Read Lamentations 1:1–5; 3:31–50 to hear how Jeremiah feels about what has happened.

Think About It

- Try to picture your city or town in ruins, with no one living in it. What would it be like?
- Jeremiah could have said, "Finally! They got what they deserved! It serves them right!" But what kind of attitude did he have instead? How do you feel when people "get what they deserve"? Why?
- Being "just" means doing what is right, being fair. God is the only completely just Person. But He is also patient and forgiving when we don't deserve it. What might happen to you if God were just but not merciful?

Go Deeper

Read Deuteronomy 32:4; Psalm 111:1–10; Lamentations 2:1–15; 3:18–30.

Prayer Starter

Think of how God has been merciful to you (such as loving you and forgiving your sins). Thank Him for that. Think also how He's been just and fair (for example, by letting your mistakes be found out before you go too far wrong). Thank Him for that too.

Facts and Fun

Knock, knock! *Who's there?*
Justice. *Justice, who?*
Justice soon as I remember, I'll tell you.

Coming Up Next:

Turning wheels, cooking pots, and an endless valley piled high with dry bones? Is this a weird dream? Or could it be *real*? Find out . . . next time!

GOD'S JUSTICE

EZEKIEL

Get set for seeing strange creatures, climbing through walls, eating a scroll, and more!

Because of their nation's sins, many Jews were captured and taken to Babylon. God chose Ezekiel, one of the captives, to set them straight. He preached while Jeremiah was prophesying similar things in Judah.

Ezekiel acts out many of his prophecies, sometimes in very strange ways. He warns the Jews that God is going to punish them by allowing their enemies to destroy Jerusalem. More Jews will be killed and taken captive. Worst of all, God will no longer dwell in a special way in the temple there—because it has been polluted by idol worship.

This is horrible news for the captives. They are losing the land God promised them through Abraham! But God also promises to be with them in Babylon and punish their enemies. Someday their descendants will return from the nations where they'll be scattered. Then Jerusalem's name will change to "The Lord Is There."

Ezekiel also foretells the coming of Israel's Messiah. Does He describe Jesus as King? Prophet? Judge? All-around nice guy? Just wait and see!

Watchman's warning

Ezekiel was captured and taken to Babylon in 597 B.C. and wrote down his prophecies from 593 to 571 B.C. He was a priest and God made him a prophet.

God calls Ezekiel a "watchman for the house of Israel" (3:17). A watchman's job is to stand guard and warn people of danger. If the watchman doesn't do his job and people are killed, then it's the watchman's fault. If a watchman warns the people and they don't do anything about it, then it's their own fault. Watchmen also let people know when "all is well." Ezekiel is able to tell God's people that someday all will be well.

Why the warning?

The people of Israel have fallen into horrible sin. Copying the pagan nations around them, they worship idols instead of God. Ezekiel warns the people about the trouble their sin will cause and assures them that someday God will save His people.

A <u>REALLY</u> AWESOME SIGHT!

You may think you've seen incredible visual effects in movies and computer games, but they're kid's stuff compared with what the prophet Ezekiel saw! Read about it in Ezekiel 1:1–28.

Think About It

- Why do you think Ezekiel spent so much time describing the four creatures? Have you ever had a hard time explaining how wonderful something was to someone who wasn't there? How would you describe a sunset over snow-covered mountains to a blind person?

- What would you do if you were before God's throne like Ezekiel? Do you think Ezekiel described everything there is about God? In what ways might God be even more awesome than Ezekiel's vision?

- The God Ezekiel wrote about is with you right now. How does that make you feel? How does that make you want to act (for example, respectfully, honestly)?

Go Deeper

Read Ezekiel 3:10–15; 10:1–22; 43:7; Daniel 7:9–10; Ephesians 3:20–21.

Prayer Starter

Try to picture the throne Ezekiel saw. Tell God how awesome He is. Ask Him to help you see clearly who He really is.

Facts and Fun

God is Father, Son, and Holy Spirit. Add four letters to the middle of the word "throne" so that it tells who sits on the throne of heaven. *(Answer: Three in one.)*

Coming Up Next:

As we leave, Ezekiel is still on his face before God. What will happen to him? Why has God shown him these wonders? Is there more? Find out . . . next time!

LUNCH WITH A PUNCH

A voice speaks and Ezekiel is suddenly pulled to his feet. What's going on? And what's that he's told to eat? Find out in Ezekiel 2:1–3:9.

Think About It

- The rebellious Israelites didn't like having God tell them what to do. How would you have felt in Ezekiel's place having to give them a message from God?
- How did God prepare Ezekiel for his tough assignment? If you knew God wanted you to do something hard like stand up to three kids twice your size, what would you do? How would you prepare for it?
- What was more important to God—that Ezekiel got results or that he obeyed? Why? What would you do if your parents told you to do something one way but you liked another way better? Why?

Go Deeper

Read Ezekiel 3:16–27; 33:1–33; Matthew 26:42; Colossians 3:17, 23.

Prayer Starter

List three things you have to do that you don't like doing. Chores? Homework? Facing up to friends when they're wrong? Ask God to help you do what you should, even when you don't feel like it.

Facts and Fun

God's words are sweet as honey to those who obey Him. How did the words God spoke through Ezekiel taste to Israel? (Answer: They stung! Like bees in the honey!)

Coming Up Next:

What message did Ezekiel bring to Israel? Who did his words sting the most? Find out . . . next time!

OBEDIENCE

OUT TO PASTURE

Have you heard of "Follow the Leader"? Here are some leaders you would *not* want to follow. Read about them and find out their fate in Ezekiel 12:1–14; 34:3–15.

Think About It
- How long would it take you to dig a hole in your bedroom wall? What would you have thought if you were Ezekiel?
- How can you tell when a leader is worth following? How would you feel if you had to follow leaders like the ones in these passages?
- Name five things that make God a good leader for you. Why do they? How can reading the Bible help you follow Him better?

Go Deeper
Read Psalm 23:1–6; Jeremiah 23:1–6; John 10:1–16.

Prayer Starter
Have you ever been lost and alone? It can be pretty scary. Disobeying God can make you feel the same way. Talk to God about following Him. Ask Him to help you obey Him so you won't get lost in sin.

Facts and Fun
How did Israel's shepherds treat their flocks? *(Answer: Baaaadly!)*

What did God tell them through Ezekiel? *(Answer: It's past-ure time.)*

Coming Up Next:
Talk about a dead audience! Find out who else Ezekiel preached to . . . next time!

PARCHED PREACHING

People are laughing . . . at God! Who was laughing, and who was to blame? What did God plan to do about it? Find out in Ezekiel 36:16, 18–29 and 37:1–14.

Think About It

- How does it feel to have someone make fun of you or your name? Why does God deserve to have everyone honor Him? How can you show respect for God and His name?
- What do you suppose Ezekiel thought when God's power brought dry bones to life? How would the things God showed Ezekiel bring honor to His name?
- If you lied a lot, acted mean, and used the names God and Jesus like bad words, what could non-Christians think about God (for example, that He was mean and dishonest)? What would they think if you were kind, honest, and respectful to others?

Go Deeper

Read Leviticus 19:12; Isaiah 29:23; Ezekiel 36:30–38; Malachi 4:2–3.

Prayer Starter

In movies, on TV, and in real life, many people use God's name without respect. Tell Him how you feel about that. What could you do to change this? Stop watching or listening when it happens? Write letters to complain? Stop buying advertiser's products? Tell God your ideas.

Facts and Fun

What happened to the dry bones when Ezekiel prophesied to them? *(Answer: They were rebone [reborn].)*

Coming Up Next:

Stand or kneel? No big deal? The choice could cost you your life! Find out why . . . next time!

GOD'S NAME

Want excitement? Danger? Mystery? Want to witness the awesome power of God? It's all in Daniel!
We're still in Babylon, a kingdom of giant idols and proud kings. Some really weird things go on here! But they are exciting because God is in control even in this foreign land.

Like Ezekiel, Daniel is a captive in Babylon. His book tells what happened while the Jews were forced to live there, and it takes place during the reigns of four kings. Two of them, Nebuchadnezzar and Belshazzar, were Babylonian. The others, Darius and Cyrus, were from Medo-Persia. God teaches these kings some pretty important lessons! But like some of us, they have to learn their lessons the hard way!

Daniel also wrote many prophecies, or predictions, of things that were to come later. The prophecies foretold the rise and fall of mighty empires and the future of God's people.

A captive sees the future!

About eight years before Ezekiel is captured, the young man Daniel, the author of this book, is taken captive to Babylon. Daniel serves in the king's palace, but wants to stay true to Jewish laws. So he refuses to eat the king's rich food. All his life, Daniel is true to God, spending much time in prayer. God gives him power to predict the future and interpret dreams. Over a period of about 60 years, he is a servant and advisor to four kings. His close friends were Shadrach, Meshach, and Abednego. He wrote the book about fifty years after Jerusalem fell in 585 B.C., but talks about events that happened during the time he served in Babylon.

The reason for the writing

Daniel wants to keep an account of the history of Babylon while the Jews are in exile there. He also writes about what God will do in the future—all the way to the end of time. Most of all, Daniel wants people to understand that God is the only God and that He has power over everything and everyone . . . even the greatest kings!

A BURNING QUESTION

What happens when a proud king doesn't get his way? He gets boiling mad and he wants others to boil too! Read about it in Daniel 3:1–28.

Think About It

- How do you think the three guys felt when they were about to be chucked into the fiery furnace? What gave them courage to stick with God?
- What would you do if you had to either worship an idol or be killed? Why? Does it matter to God what you decide? How do you know?
- If you knew that God might not save your life, would you still want to do things His way? What could help you be strong?

Go Deeper

Read Psalm 33:18–22; 62:5–8; Daniel 1:1–21; Philippians 4:13.

Prayer Starter

Don't forget: The same God who protected the men in the fiery furnace lives in you. Talk to God about how hard it is to do things His way sometimes, like when friends are doing wrong things. Ask for help to stand firm and trust Him no matter what happens.

Facts and Fun

Nothing is fireproof, not even rock. (Think of lava!) But God can do anything. So He made Shadrach, Meshach, and Abednego fireproof, and the flames melted Nebuchadnezzar's stony, prideful heart . . . for a while.

Coming Up Next:

What do a proud king and wild oxen have in common? What do kings do when they go bonkers? Find out . . . next time!

A BEASTLY SITUATION

Pride can get a person into a lot of trouble. Even after seeing God's awesome power at work, Nebuchadnezzar still didn't get it. Find out how God taught him a lesson he *wouldn't* forget! Read Daniel 4:1–9, 18–37.

Think About It

- Picture yourself eating grass and living like an animal. How does it feel? How does it taste?
- What was wrong with Nebuchadnezzar taking credit for his mighty kingdom? How might things have been different if he had humbly recognized that God helped him?
- Nebuchadnezzar eventually realized that he got the strength to live, breathe, and do everything else from God. What are three reasons it is important to remember that everything good in your life comes from God (for example, it helps you trust God)?

Go Deeper

Read Psalm 29:1–2; Proverbs 11:12; 16:18; Daniel 4:10–17; John 15:5.

Prayer Starter

Think about all your talents and the neat things you've been able to do. Then remind yourself that God has helped you to do them. You can't even breathe without God! Isn't He wonderful? Talk to Him about it.

Facts and Fun

People cannot really eat grass. Our bodies are not designed to digest its tough fibers. So God must have kept Nebuchadnezzar alive in a miraculous way!

Coming Up Next:

What is it with Babylon and proud kings? Is this the nation of big egos? Find out about spooky goings-on in the castle . . . next time!

HUMILITY

THE MYSTERIOUS MESSAGE

King Belshazzar was hosting a drunken banquet and everyone was whooping it up. That is, until a headless, almost bodiless visitor crashed the party! Read about it in Daniel 5:1–31.

Think About It
- How would you have felt at King Belshazzar's table that night? Why was it wrong to praise the gods of gold and silver, bronze and iron, wood and stone? Why doesn't it even make sense to worship them?
- What lesson did Belshazzar fail to learn from his father?
- What comes first in your life? Family? Friends? TV? Sports? Computer games? Homework? (Didn't think so!) What three things can you do to put God first (for example, set aside regular time to spend with Him)?

Go Deeper
Read Exodus 20:1–6; Jeremiah 10:3–5, 10–12; Daniel 1:1–2; 2:1–49.

Prayer Starter
Talk to God about what's important to you and why. Be honest, even if praying and reading the Bible are not your favorite activities right now. Ask for help to remember Him all the time and want to make Him most important in your life.

Facts and Fun
Belshazzar couldn't see the writing on the wall. So God gave him a hand.

Coming Up Next:
Meet a king who wanted people to *pray* to him like a god! Find out why Daniel wouldn't say "Amen" to that . . . next time!

HUNGER STRIKE

Being jealous can make people do stupid and mean things—
but who gets it in the end? Find out in Daniel 6:1–23.

Think About It
- King Darius was forced to follow the decree (law) he made. Why do you think he signed the paper that the leaders of Babylon wrote for him? What should he have done before making his decision?
- After Darius' experience, how do you feel about making hasty promises? Why?
- How do you feel when someone breaks a promise to you? Why? Why is it important to keep your promises?

Go Deeper
Read Psalm 91:1–16; Matthew 5:37; James 5:12.

Prayer Starter
In what ways has God helped you learn to trust Him? Does He help you when you're afraid? When you're taking tests? When things seem to be going all haywire? Is it hard or easy for you to trust God? Talk to Him about it and about becoming more trustworthy yourself.

Facts and Fun
The administrators and satraps wanted Daniel's hide.
So they lied.
But their reward for lyin' was Lion . . .
Jaws-t what they deserved! (Daniel 6:24)

Coming Up Next:
What if your best friend kept turning on you but you had to stay friends because God told you to? Read about it . . . next time!

MINOR PROPHETS

An army that *never* gets enough to eat, a prophet who tries to hide from God, and some pretty rotten cousins is what you'll find in the Minor Prophets. These men may be in the minor league (because their books are short), but they have major messages for God's people.

"Turn around. Follow God before it's too late!" is the major message of the Minor Prophets, speaking to rebellious people. They also tell of the suffering in store for those who keep sinning. The people kept running after *man-made* gods (idols) instead of worshiping the God who *made* man. And guess what? They had major problems with nasty neighbors as God let them experience the results of their sin.

These books are not all gloom and doom, however.

They also give wonderful pictures of God's love and patience, and promises for the future when God's Messiah will put things right. Today, we have a head start because the Messiah, Jesus, and the Holy Spirit help us obey God.

Twelve unusual guys

About 300 years after Solomon

Obadiah, 853–796 B.C.: Prophesied against Edom, a nasty neighbor.

Joel, 853–796 B.C.: Lived in Judah or Jerusalem. The hungry army guy.

Jonah, 800–750 B.C.: On special assignment to Nineveh. Did *not* want to go!

Amos, 792–753 B.C.: Shepherd. Before exile, predicted return from exile!

Isaiah is in business

Micah, 750–686 B.C.: From Moresheth in Judah. "The Messiah will be born in Bethlehem."

Hosea, 753–715 B.C.: From Israel. Spoke of God's love even through betrayal.

No more Isaiah. King Josiah reigns.

Nahum, 663–612 B.C.: From Elkosh. "Nineveh will fall."

Habakkuk, 663–597 B.C.: From Judah. Asked God a *lot* of questions.

Zephaniah, 640–609 B.C.: From Judah. Possible descendant of King Hezekiah. Warned about coming defeat and exile.

Jerusalem conquered. People carried into exile in Babylon. Daniel's an *old* man.

Haggai, 520 B.C.: Preached in Jerusalem. "Rebuild the temple."

Zechariah, 520–480 B.C.: Born in Babylon. Preached in Jerusalem. Prophesied about the Messiah.

Malachi, 433–430 B.C.: Preached in Jerusalem. Spoke of the gifts God loves.

Turn back or else!

The theme of most of these books is "Turn back to God." Otherwise the people will have to suffer the bad results of their sins. The book of Jonah is the only one written like a story. It tells about God's mercy to the evil city Nineveh, the Israelites' enemy. The prophets also wrote to encourage the people that God has a plan and will make everything turn out all right eventually. The Israelites had hard, sinful hearts, which made it difficult for them to follow God. But God knew that by sending Jesus to die for us, our hearts could be soft again, ready and willing to obey Him.

REAL LOVE DOESN'T QUIT

God loved the Kingdom of Judah, but couldn't trust her people. They ran after other gods like an unfaithful wife who kept betraying her husband. What did God do? Find out in Hosea 1:2; 4:1–9; 5:9–15; 14:1–9.

Think About It

- If your best friend forgot you existed every time a new friend came around, how would you feel? Why do you think Judah kept following other gods? How do you think God felt?
- The people of Judah deserved to be punished for their sins, but God warned them and promised to forgive and heal them. Why? Why didn't He just give up on them?
- Before Jesus' death, everyone had hard sinful hearts. How do you think being a Christian now is different from being one of God's people then?
- God never gives up on you. Never, ever! (Hebrews 13:5) How is He even better than a best friend?

Go Deeper

Read Psalm 86:15; 89:30–33; 100:5; Isaiah 25:1; Hosea 6:1–6; 10:12.

Prayer Starter

Tell God about your friends, and talk to Him about being a friend who doesn't quit. With God, think of ways you can show your friends what kind of friend God can be.

Facts and Fun

Plucking daisies:
God: Judah loves Me. She loves Me not. She loves Me. She loves Me not. . . .

   Judah: God loves me. He loves me! HE loves me! HE loves ME! HE *LOVES* ME!

Coming Up Next:

What kind of terrible, unstoppable army *eats* its way to your door? Find out . . . next time!

MARCH, MUNCH, MARCH ◆ ◆ ◆

Locust swarms! Grasshopper invasion! Black storm clouds!
There's a mighty army coming. Watch out! Make sure it's
not coming after *you!* Read about it in Joel 2:1–25.

Think About It

- How would you feel if you saw all your food being eaten
  by millions of grasshopper-like bugs? How would you try
  to stop them? What did God want His people to do?
- Why did God let the army loose? What difference does it
  make when people stop doing evil and God steps in?
- Why isn't just saying you're sorry enough? How can you
  show you mean it (for example, by obeying next time, by
  fixing what you broke . . .)?

Go Deeper

Read Ezekiel 18:30–32; Joel 1:1–20; 2:26–32; Luke 15:7;
1 John 1:9.

Prayer Starter

God doesn't expect us to be perfect overnight, but when we
do things we know are wrong He expects us to talk to Him
about it and grow past it. It's hard to admit when we're
wrong. Tell God how you feel about apologizing when you
do bad things. Ask for help with your attitude and for
forgiveness and help.

Facts and Fun

Locust swarms can have billions of insects with about 20
million per square mile. A single swarm can cover 80 square
miles or more![1] They're not picky. They eat almost any
plant! Want to know more? Check out any encyclopedia.

Coming Up Next:

While Judah was getting beaten and eaten, what was
happening to the northern kingdom of Israel? Find out . . .
next time!

1. University of Florida Book of Insect Records: http://gnv.ifas.ufl.edu/~tjw/recbk.htm

WE'RE DOIN' JUST FINE—<u>NOT!</u>

The rich northern kingdom of Israel thought they had it made.
Did they forget something? Read Amos 4:6–12; 5:1–15; 9:11–15.

Think About It

- "Cows of Bashan" were first-rate cows that were spoiled rotten.
  Amos was saying how rich the people were then. If you had
  everything you wanted like Israel did at this point, what would
  you talk to God about?
- Israel forgot about God, because they had more than enough of
  everything. So He got their attention by taking everything away.
  When do you think it's easiest to forget about God? Why do you
  suppose many people only remember God when trouble comes?
- People who pray mainly during trouble often stop when their
  trouble stops. They aren't in the habit of including God in their
  everyday lives. What three things can you do to stay in the
  habit of including God?

Go Deeper

Read 1 Chronicles 16:8–13; Psalm 63:3–6; 143:5; Amos 2:6–16.

Prayer Starter

What five things could have gone wrong lately, but didn't? Almost
miss the bus, spill your drink, forget your homework? Talk to God
about how well He cares for you. Ask Him to help you remember
Him in the good times and to include Him in your life every day.

Facts and Fun

Did you know that part of Amos's prophecy in chapter nine is coming
true right now? Since 1948, Jews have been returning to Israel from all
over the world. They have been able to make the deserts bloom by
using irrigation. Where there was once dry land, there is now enough
food grown to export to other countries! It's great to see God's Word
coming true. And there is much more to come!

Coming Up Next:

Remember the brothers Jacob and Esau? Well, their descendants
had a really *bad* family feud going! Read about it . . . next time!

TAKE THAT!

The Edomites, descendants of Jacob's brother Esau, thought they were really something. They enjoyed seeing their cousins in Judah and Israel getting captured and killed. They even helped their enemies! Find out what God thought about *that* in Obadiah 1:1–21 and Malachi 1:1–5.

Think About It
- Jacob and Esau didn't get along well and neither did their descendants. What punishment did the Edomites get for not defending their relatives? What do you think they should have done when their cousins were in trouble? Why?
- Think of someone you're around a lot (like your brother or sister or a best friend). How do you get along with that person? What two things can you do to make things even nicer?

Go Deeper
Read Psalm 137:7; Jeremiah 49:7–22; Romans 12:10; 1 John 2:9–11; 3:10.

Prayer Starter
How do you act and feel when someone else gets into trouble for talking back or forgetting to do a chore or his or her homework? (Are you relieved? Glad? Sad?) Talk to God about it. Pray for the right attitude and for ways to help out.

Facts and Fun
EDOMMODE: prideful Edom looking in a mirror.
FRIENDINNEEDOM: what Edom should have been.
EDOOM: Edom after God got through with it.
REDOM: what you should do with books of the Bible.

Coming Up Next:
First the people don't listen to their prophets! Now even a prophet disobeys God! Sound fishy? Find out . . . next time!

YOU CAN RUN, BUT YOU CAN'T HIDE

Fugitive! Man on the run! Who's hiding? Why? Will he get away with it? Find out in Jonah 1:1–17; 2:1, 10; 3:1–5.

Think About It

- What would you do for three days inside a fish? (Whine? Count ribs? Eat seafood?) What do you think God was telling Jonah through this strange experience?
- Why is it impossible to hide from God?
- Have you ever tried to run away from something you didn't want to do, but then you got caught? What happened? What's a better thing to do? Why?

Go Deeper

Read Job 34:22; Psalm 31:19–20; 32:7; 139:1–16; Jonah 2:2–9; 3:6–10.

Prayer Starter

You can't hide *from* God, but you can hide *with* Him! Find a special place where you can be alone with God. Some people pray in a closet. You might find a place under the stairs, in the backyard, or up in a tree. (Just make sure your place is safe and that someone can find you in an emergency!)

Facts and Fun

Did you know that someone was found alive inside a whale? His name was James Bartley and he was in the whale's stomach for a day and a half in 1891! He came out bleached white! What do you think his favorite Bible story was afterwards?

Coming Up Next:

Want to read about an incredible land where the weak become strong and there's no fear or war? Find out about it . . . next time!

GUILT

WHO CAN YOU TRUST?

Warning! God's people are about to suffer greatly for their stubbornness. Sure, God loves them, but will He rescue them *this* time? Find out in Micah 2:1–7; 4:1–8; 5:1–2; 7:18–20.

Think About It

- The people preferred the false prophets' lies instead of the truth that Micah told. Why? Who would you have believed? Why? Who do you find it easier to listen to? Parents and teachers or your friends? Why?
- Even though God hates sin, how does He feel about sinners? How do you know?
- Sometimes love has to be tough. How did God show tough love? Why was it necessary? How does this passage also show God's gentle love?

Go Deeper

Read Job 37:13; Psalm 103:8–14; Micah 1:1–9; 2:8–3:12; Zephaniah 3:17.

Prayer Starter

Tell God how you feel about getting punished. What's bad about it? What's good? Ask Him to help you understand about tough love.

Facts and Fun

Read this aloud to hear what it's really saying: Thee udder prof fits maid peephole go as tray, sewed hay add two deep end on Micah a loan to tail that Ruth. Sum daisies head, "Indian their wheel beep piece Ann gnome or wore." Water grate thyme toe bee all hive!

Coming Up Next:

There was once an empire that was *so* cruel and evil that it made the whole world tremble. Find out its fate . . . next time!

THE VERDICT: GUILTY!

In Nahum's time, the Assyrians ruled the world. Their capital was Nineveh and they were the cruelest people alive! Then God finally had enough! Find out what happened in Nahum 1:1–9; 2:1–10; 3:16–19.

Think About It
- The Bible says that God doesn't anger easily. What do you think it takes to make God really angry? How does it feel to read about God being furious? Why?
- God's type of anger is called righteous anger. Why do you think it's called that? How do you think it's different from sinful anger? When could you feel righteous anger?

Go Deeper
Read Psalm 7:8–17; 10:1–18; Nahum 1:10–15; 2:11–13; 3:1–4; Ephesians 4:26, 31.

Prayer Starter
Do you need help to know when your anger is good or bad? Tell God about it. Getting angry because someone does or says things you don't like or because things aren't going your way is not God's type of anger. Talk to Him about things or people that make you angry. He'll understand. Ask for help to be patient and kind instead.

Facts and Fun
What's the difference between being mad and being angry? Mad means "insane"; angry means "upset." Eating grass like King Nebuchadnezzar is mad. Mad can also mean "being foolish," like buying a car without driving it. Mad dogs have rabies, not tempers. People often say "mad" when they mean "angry," but don't tell your English teacher you're mad. She may believe you!

Coming Up Next:
A prophet has the nerve to complain to God! Do you think God puts up with that? Find out what happens . . . next time!

COMPLAINER BONES

Ever wonder why rotten people who do bad things seem to get away with it? Habakkuk did. Read Habakkuk's complaints, and God's answers, in Habakkuk 1:1–13; 2:1–3; 3:17–18.

Think About It

- How do you feel when things seem unfair? What do you *do*? We know that God eventually works everything out right (Habakkuk 2:2–3). How does that make you feel?
- What do you think Habakkuk would complain to God about if he were here today? What do you think God would answer? Why?
- Why do you think Habakkuk could say what he did in 3:17–19? Could you trust God if there were no food in the house and no money to buy it? Why or why not?

Go Deeper

Read Psalm 37:1–40; Proverbs 23:17–18; Habakkuk 1:14–17; 2:4, 12–14; 3:1–16.

Prayer Starter

Be honest with God, while still being respectful. Tell Him about what you think is unfair. Has someone else received praise that you deserved? Have you been punished for what another person did wrong? Ask for help to understand what's happening. Thank Him ahead of time for eventually working everything out right and ask for help to trust Him to do that, even when you don't understand.

Facts and Fun

Find out what Habakkuk learned by taking him out of the picture. (Cross out HABAKKUK. What's left?):

HABGAKKUKOHABAKKUKHABAKDKIUKHABAKSKUK
HABIAKKUKHNABAKKUCKHAOBAKKUKNHABAK
TRKOUKHLABAKKUK *(Answer: God is in control.)*

Coming Up Next:

Uh-oh! God's really angry now. Find out why . . . next time!

DD-DAY (DESTRUCTION AND DELIVERANCE DAY)!

What happens after all God's warnings have failed and He's finally had enough: people's sin is just too much? The great Day of the Lord is coming! Read about it in Zephaniah 1:1–7; 2:1–3; 3:1–13.

Think About It

- God didn't have much good to say about *anyone* in the book of Zephaniah. Why was that? Why do you think God decided to put a stop to the horrible evil the people were doing?
- God corrects those He loves. Sometimes He has to let them suffer the consequences of their sins. Then maybe they'll do what's right next time. If you've been punished for doing wrong, how does it effect the way you think about doing it again?
- When we become Christians, God replaces our hard hearts with soft ones. Why is a soft heart better? Disobeying God can make your heart hard toward Him. Name five other things that could make your heart hard. Name five things that can keep it soft.

Go Deeper

Read Ezekiel 11:19–20; Zephaniah 1:8–18; Ephesians 4:17–18; Hebrews 3:12–13.

Prayer Starter

God loved His people, but they didn't love Him or obedience would have been easy. They were caught up in selfish wants and payed no attention to God. Pray for help to love God, keep your heart soft, and know what's right. Ask for strength to do right.

Facts and Fun

Why were Jerusalem's officials "like roaring lions"? (*Answer: They lived in their pride.*)

Why were her rulers "like evening wolves"? (*Answer: They ate. Then came mourning.*)

Coming Up Next:

What does a pile of old rubble have to do with God's plans for His people? Find out . . . next time!

REBUILD RUBBLE!

What can you build from a pile of rubble? A fort to play in? A shack? A castle? Find out what God wanted built in Haggai 1:1–15 and 2:1–9.

Think About It
- Imagine that your church is lying in ruins. All that's left are piles of bricks, stones, and wood. But no one cares and nobody wants to help rebuild it. How do you think God would feel?
- Why do you think God was upset that the people hadn't rebuilt the temple?
- The temple represented God's presence with His people. Why do you think God wanted rebuilding the temple to be a priority?
- How can you put God first when you choose what movie to watch or what game to play? When you have extra time? When someone needs help? What other ways can you put Him first?

Go Deeper
Read Ezra 3:8–13; Haggai 2:15–19; Matthew 6:31–33; John 6:27; Colossians 3:23.

Prayer Starter
Talk to God about your hobbies and activities. Tell Him why they're important to you. Ask Him to help you understand what's important to Him and how you can help. Pray about ways to volunteer at church. Then keep your eyes open: He may give you a chance to help others too.

Facts and Fun
What's the only house that's smaller than the one who lives inside? *(Answer: A heart with God living in it!)*

Coming Up Next:
How can a city make a U-turn? Where will it lead? Find out . . . next time!

MANY HAPPY RETURNS

Jerusalem is full of broken walls and smashed houses! So who is this happy prophet standing in the rubble saying how great things can be? Find out in Zechariah 1:1–6 and 8:1–17.

Think About It
- Zechariah foretold a good future and predicted the coming of the Messiah. How do you think the people felt when they heard the news? Why?
- What would you do if you were told that all your secret dreams and hopes would come true?
- Zechariah knew good things come out of tough times. Name three challenges that lead to good things (a close soccer game has the best victory, fixing problems with a friend makes your friendship stronger). Do you think God wants these things for you? Why or why not?

Go Deeper
Read Psalm 130:7; Zechariah 1:7–17; 2:1–5, 10–13; Ephesians 3:20–21.

Prayer Starter
What "smashed houses" do you have right now? Problems at home or school? How could God use them for good? Talk to God about them. Ask for hope and faith that He will use them for good. Thank Him for knowing what's best.

Facts and Fun
Match prophecies of Zechariah to events in the Gospels.

1. I will live with you (2:10)
2. Your King will come on a donkey (9:9)
3. Thirty pieces of silver (11:12–13)

a. Judas (Matthew 27:3–10)
b. The Word became flesh (John 1:14)
c. Hosanna! (Matthew 21:1–9)

(Answers: 1. b; 2. c; 3. a)

Coming Up Next:
How would you like to open a gift and find garbage inside? What gives? Find out . . . next time!

I LOVE YOU WITH HALF OF MY HEART

The temple had been rebuilt, and the people were offering sacrifices again. Well, sort of . . . So why wasn't God pleased? Find out in Malachi 1:1–14; 3:6–12.

Think About It
- The most important person in the world is visiting you. How would he or she feel being welcomed with hand-me-down, broken gifts? How is that like what Judah gave to God?
- If you had two things for your mother and one was broken, which would you give her? Why? What did the gifts the people gave God say about how they felt about Him?
- God loves one who gives out of a heart of love. What gifts would you like to give God? Why? Name three "whole heart" gifts you can give such as love, obedience, or belief.

Go Deeper
Read Deuteronomy 6:5; Malachi 2:1–9; 3:13–4:6; Matthew 23:23; Mark 12:33.

Prayer Starter
If someone gave you the right half of a heart-shaped Valentine, it would look more like a question mark than a heart. When we give God only half our hearts, do we really love Him? Tell God what you think about that. Ask Him for help to find ways to give cheerfully to Him and others.

Facts and Fun
What's ten percent of everything? *(Answer: God's.)*

What's 100 percent of everything? *(Answer: God's.)*

If you multiply zero by 50 million, add 10 percent, and divide by half, what do you get? *(Answer: A whole lot of nothing.)*

Coming Up Next:
After centuries of silence, God suddenly surprises everyone by keeping a promise. Read about it . . . next time!

THE GOSPELS: MATTHEW & MARK

I t is finally time! Prophecies are about to be fulfilled, and the most radical time in the whole Bible is about to begin. Get ready to walk, sail, and go fishing—for more than just fish! Have you ever watched someone stand on water that wasn't ice? Heard a voice coming from out of nowhere? Seen someone changed before your eyes? You will in the gospels of Matthew and Mark.

Gospel means "good news," and the good news was Jesus. Matthew's gospel contains lots of Jesus' words, including His famous Sermon on the Mount and many of His parables—stories that teach a lesson.

Mark's gospel tells about more of the things Jesus did than any other gospel. One thing you'll notice is that Jesus and His disciples move around a lot. Some really exciting things take place on their trips. Wherever Jesus goes, wonderful things happen. Just wait. The adventures are only beginning!

You can believe these guys!

Matthew, the author of the first gospel, was a tax collector and became one of Jesus' twelve disciples. The Jews hated tax collectors because they helped the Roman rulers. Matthew became a good man after knowing Jesus. His gospel is a firsthand account of someone who saw it all.

The author of the second gospel is John Mark. Peter, another apostle, was Mark's close friend. In this gospel, Mark wrote down a lot of Peter's stories about Jesus, so his is a secondhand account. But it is a short, action-packed gospel!

Matthew and Mark both wrote their gospels 20 to 40 years after Jesus' return to heaven.

Why were these books written?

Matthew wrote to show that Jesus fulfills the Old Testament prophecies, proving He is the Messiah predicted long ago by the prophets. Most things foretold about the Messiah happen during Jesus' life. (The rest of the prophecies will be fulfilled when He returns.)

Mark likes action. He tells the story of Jesus with lots of details about what Jesus did during His time on earth. He wants everyone to understand how Jesus served others and sacrificed Himself for them.

A STARRING ROLE

How did a poor carpenter's family go from sawdust to star-dust and get a major role in the history of mankind? Read about it in Matthew 1:18–2:12.

Think About It
- If you were looking for a newborn king today, where would you look? Why do you think God chose a stable for His Son's birth?
- How should a heavenly king be different from an earthly king? Why? What would make you obey and honor such a king?
- What gift would you have given to Jesus? Why? What can you give Him now?

Go Deeper
Read Micah 5:2; Matthew 2:13–23; Luke 22:25–30; 23:42; John 18:36–37.

Prayer Starter
Even though the wise men might have been rich and powerful, they knew they should bow down and worship Jesus, a poor child. We know that Jesus is the greatest King of all. What gift would you like to give your King now? Some time? A song? Your heart? Tell Him about it.

Facts and Fun
Have you ever sung the Christmas carol "We Three Kings of Orient Are"? It's a great song, but no one knows for sure how many wise men there were or exactly where they came from. The Bible doesn't say!

Coming Up Next:
Find out what happens when the Child grows up and meets His worst, most hateful enemy face to face . . . next time!

OUTSMARTING THE ENEMY

Out in the rocky, dusty deserts of Judea, there's a face-off between Satan and Jesus. Who will win? Find out in Matthew 3:1–2, 13–4:11, 23–25.

Think About It

- How do you think Jesus felt while being tempted? How would you have felt? Why?
- Why didn't Jesus just tell the Devil to go away? Do you think that would have made the devil leave? Why or why not?
- The Devil tried to use scripture to trick Jesus, but it didn't work. Why not? What can you do to follow Jesus' example and make sure you aren't fooled?

Go Deeper

Read Psalm 119:11, 105; Ephesians 6:10–17; 2 Timothy 3:16–17.

Prayer Starter

How important is the Bible to you? Would you like to be able to fight off temptation with scripture the way Jesus did? Talk to God about it.

Facts and Fun

When Jesus quoted scripture, He only quoted the Old Testament, because the New Testament wasn't written yet. Today, we have even more scripture to help us. In order to fight temptation with scripture, though, we have to know what the Bible says. Although parts of the Bible have been translated into over 2,200 languages, 440 million people still have no scripture in their language at all!

Coming Up Next:

Eating bugs, getting wet, and fishing for people? What gives? Find out . . . next time!

GONE FISHING

The Devil attacks Him in the desert, His friend John disappears into a dungeon, and Jesus is just getting *started*! Read all about it in Mark 1:1–20!

Think About It

- What would it take for you to drop everything and leave your family and friends? Peter and Andrew left their nets "at once." Jesus must have been quite a person to convince the disciples to follow Him so readily! Name three times you obeyed God "at once" by listening to your parents or following your conscience.

- What matters to you most? If God asked you to, would you give up your favorite toy or game, quit hanging around certain friends, or visit a sick neighbor? What kinds of things have you already done for God? Name three.

Go Deeper

Read Joshua 24:15; Mark 1:21–2:28; John 10:27; 12:26.

Prayer Starter

Talk to God about how hard it is to follow Him sometimes. Ask Him to help you care more about what He wants for you than what you want for yourself. Believe it or not, you'll be happier when you let Him run things!

Facts and Fun

Peter and Andrew left their nets immediately. In fact, the Gospel of Mark uses the Greek word for "immediately" 42 times![2] Mark must have been in a hurry to tell the good news about Jesus. His is the shortest of the four Gospels.

Coming Up Next:

Did you know that Jesus gave us a recipe for happiness? You'll be shocked when you hear the ingredients . . . next time!

---

2. Notes by Philip Yancey and Tim Stafford, *The Student Bible*, New International Version (Grand Rapids, Michigan, 1990), page 874.

WHAT'S COOKIN'!

Mix one cup of hunger, one tablespoon of persecution, two cups of tears . . . hey, is this the right recipe? Find out in Matthew 5:1–16, 38–48.

Think About It

- Some listeners probably thought Jesus was crazy. If you had been on that hill, what would you have thought?
- How does what Jesus taught compare to what society tells us is right today? (For example, we're told to get even, not be peacemakers.) Why do you think it takes more courage to do things Jesus' way?
- How do you think people can be blessed (made holy and happy) in the middle of mourning or persecution? How is God's recipe for joy different from most people's ideas?
- If you do what Jesus said, where will your heart be focused? Think of three ways you can follow what Jesus taught here; for example, how can you keep things peaceful at home?

Go Deeper

Read Exodus 20:1–17; Matthew 5:17–37; Ephesians 2:8–10; James 1:2, 12.

Prayer Starter

Think about God's "recipe for joy" and about your life. Are you happy or blessed in these ways? Talk to God about how you can be and ask for His help.

Facts and Fun

When life is too easy, our faith gets weak. Christians who are persecuted—treated badly for believing in Jesus—usually have very strong faith. Because they know that faith grows stronger with trouble, many pray for persecution to come to America and other prosperous countries! So look out!

Coming Up Next:

Hold it! What's that in your eye? A two-by-four? How did *that* happen? Find out . . . next time!

PULL THE PLANK!

Poke. Yank. Hold still! I've almost got it. Oops! Find out what's wrong in Matthew 6:1–14; 7:1–5, 24–29.

Think About It

- What did Jesus mean by saying to take the plank out of your eye before helping someone else remove a speck of sawdust? What attitude was He talking about getting rid of?
- Do other people's habits bug you? How do you like someone clicking their chewing gum in your ear? Poking you repeatedly in the ribs? Talking to you with a mouth full of mashed potatoes and broccoli? What do you do that might bug someone else? What can you do about it?
- Would you rather look good to people or to God? Why? How can this affect your actions (for example, do you talk respectfully to your parents and elders or "mouth off" to be "in" with a cool group)?

Go Deeper

Read Proverbs 17:3; 21:2; Matthew 6:15–34; 7:6–23; Romans 2:1; 14:10; 1 Corinthians 4:5.

Prayer Starter

Talk to God about the real you. Is it different from what others see? God knows you inside out, so you can tell Him anything. Go ahead.

Facts and Fun

Mixed-up fun:
When you see your own faults, what do you get?

AELCR NIIOVS

(Answer: CLEAR VISION)

Coming Up Next:

What on earth could amaze the Son of God? How did a Roman soldier astonish Jesus? Find out . . . next time!

ON CALL

What's with all the sick people? Hundreds of them! Is there an epidemic? Find out in Matthew 8:1–16; 9:18–33.

Think About It

- The centurion was an important leader in the Roman army. Most Jews hated the Romans, and Jesus was Jewish. Why do you think the centurion turned to Him when he needed help?
- Jesus was amazed by the centurion's faith. How can you be like the centurion?
- What do you think it would have been like to watch Jesus healing everyone who came to Him? Would that have increased your faith? Why or why not? Since you were not there to see it, does reading about Jesus' power to heal help your faith now? Why or why not?

Go Deeper

Read Matthew 8:17–9:17; Mark 6:56; James 5:14–15.

Prayer Starter

Jesus cared about all the people who came to Him for healing. Tell Him about someone you know who is sick and ask Him to help. If no one is sick, then tell Him what makes you feel better when you're not feeling well.

Facts and Fun

Even though modern medicine helps make people well and makes it possible for us to live longer, all healing really comes from God (Exodus 15:26, Psalm 103:3–4).

Coming Up Next:

Why would Jesus send His twelve disciples away? Did they do something wrong? Find out . . . next time!

HEAVEN SENT

Where will the disciples go? Why can't they take their suitcases? What devious dangers are lurking ahead? Find out in Matthew 9:35–10:20.

Think About It

- If you'd been a disciple, how would you have felt being sent off? How would you have felt leaving without any money or extra clothes? Why? Why do you think Jesus didn't go with them?
- How did sending the disciples out help Jesus take care of all the people who needed His help? How is that like missionaries today?
- Where do you see a "plentiful harvest" that needs picking? (Friends or relatives who don't know Jesus? At school?) How can you help the Lord of the Harvest right where you live (for example, tell people about Jesus, bake someone a cake, or fix a bike)?

Go Deeper

Read Isaiah 44:8; Matthew 10:21–42; 24:14; 28:18–20; Acts 1:8.

Prayer Starter

Tell God how you feel about talking to others about Him. Is it easy? Hard? In between? Tell Him what makes you feel that way. Ask for help and courage if you need it.

Facts and Fun

The Bible tells us that before Jesus returns, the good news of the gospel will be preached in every tribe and nation. And that means people who speak 6,858[3] different languages!

Coming Up Next:

The Pharisees hate Jesus and they're out to trap Him! Can He outsmart them? Find out . . . next time!

3. Wycliffe Bible Translators: http://www.wycliffe.org/wbt/usa/TranGoal.htm

MERCY RULES!

When are grainfields and shriveled hands dangerous? When they're used as traps! Read about it in Matthew 11:25–30 and 12:1–13.

Think About It

- What would you have done if you'd seen Jesus zap the man's hand back into shape? Jesus turned the Pharisees' traps around. What was more important than their strict rules? Why?
- Mercy is great kindness. How did Jesus show God's mercy in this passage? How has God shown mercy in your life? (Protected you? Given you a great family?)
- Why do you think the Pharisees were so picky about Sabbath rules? Jesus felt differently because of His different priorities. What was most important to Him? Why? What gave Him the right to feel that way?

Go Deeper

Read Zechariah 7:9; Matthew 9:13; 11:1–24; 12:14–45; James 2:12–13.

Prayer Starter

Think of three ways God has shown mercy to you, such as forgiving you or keeping you safe even when you disobeyed. Ask Him to help you learn how to be merciful, too.

Facts and Fun

Most of the Old Testament was written in Hebrew, which is read from right to left. Read the sentence below like Hebrew and find out why mercy rules.

‚DROL eht ot sknaht evig ‚hO"

".reverof serudne ycrem siH roF !doog si eH rof

VJKN 43:61 selcinorhC 1

Coming Up Next:

The grouchy, rule-keeping Pharisees had sharp stingers, but did those pests scare Jesus? Read all about it . . . next time!

STAND WHERE THEY CAN SEE YOU

Jesus was doing His job. But the problem was that it was rubbing some very powerful people the wrong way. Read about it in Mark 3:1–19, 31–35.

Think About It

- If you had been there, what would you have said to the people who would rather see a man suffer than break a rule?
- Why was Jesus angry with the Pharisees? Why do you think He told the man with the shriveled hand to stand in front of everyone instead of healing him in private?
- Jesus was bold even though many people thought He was wrong—or crazy. Is it harder for you to do what's right when others are watching you? Why or why not?
- Why do you think Jesus called those who do God's will His family? What's the family resemblance?

Go Deeper

Read Joshua 1:9; Proverbs 28:1; Matthew 7:21; Mark 4:1–41; Acts 4:13, 16–20.

Prayer Starter

Talk to God about what it's like to be the only one standing up for what's right. Ask Him to help you be bold like Jesus—even if other people think you're crazy!

Facts and Fun

The Bible records 35 miracles[4] Jesus performed, but according to the apostle John, all the books in the world couldn't contain all the wonderful, miraculous things He did (John 21:25).

Coming Up Next:

Where would you look to find the greatest treasure in the world? In a sunken ship? A Pharaoh's tomb? Find out . . . next time!

4. New American Standard *Ryrie Study Bible*, Expanded Edition, (Chicago, Moody Press, 1995), page 1502

HIDDEN TREASURE!

What do seeds, weeds, and enormous pearls have in common? Read all about it in Matthew 13:1–9, 18–30, and 44–46.

Think About It
- Lots of people dream of finding buried treasure. What would you like to find? What would you be willing to do to discover it?
- Why do you think the treasure and pearl were worth so much to the people who found them? What would something have to be like for you to give everything for it?
- Think about how much you love God. How can spending time with Him and reading the Bible be like finding buried treasure? What is it worth to you? Enough to give Him time, choose His way, avoid bad actions and words? What?

Go Deeper
Read Matthew 6:33; 13:10–17, 31–43, 47–58; Luke 14:26; John 6:35.

Prayer Starter
Talk to God about what you'd be willing to give up for Him. Be honest. He knows what you're thinking anyway. Ask Him to help you love Him more than anything.

Facts and Fun
The largest pearl ever found is called the Pearl of Lao-Tze.[5] It came from a giant clam, weighs forty pounds, and is worth more than 40 million dollars! How's that for a pearl of great price?

Coming Up Next:
One stormy night the disciples see a ghost! Or *do* they? Find out . . . next time!

5. The Bead Site, Center for Bead Research: http://www.thebeadsite.com/REC-PRL.html

POWERFUL STUFF!

Unbelievable things were happening out on the waves! Were the disciples seeing things? Find out by reading Matthew 14:13–33 and 16:13–17.

Think About It

- If you had eaten some of that special bread and fish, what might you have thought about Jesus?
- Like Peter, have you ever stepped out of your comfort zone and tried to do something you thought maybe wouldn't work? What was it? What happened?
- How could Jesus do the miracles He did? What made Him different from every other person? How do His miracles help you understand that He is both God and Man? So what does that mean? (Can you trust Him? Believe what He said? What?)

Go Deeper

Read Matthew 14:1–12, 34–16:12; John 1:1–3; 5:19–21; 10:30; 14:11.

Prayer Starter

Talk to Jesus about His miracles. Tell Him how you feel about His incredible power. Tell Him how you feel about knowing He is God (powerful) and Man (understands you).

Facts and Fun

When Jesus and Peter walked on water, it was a miracle. People can't walk on water unless it's frozen into ice, but there are two kinds of insects and about 15 types of spiders that can.[6] The water strider is an insect that appears to be skating on water. When a water spider races across the water its eight legs hardly seem to touch it.

Coming up Next:

There's a real crazy man loose! He snaps iron chains like paper! And he's bad, bad, bad! Read about it . . . next time!

6. "Walking on Water" http://whyfiles.news.wisc.edu/shorties/walk_on_water.html

WILD MAN

One man Jesus met was downright scary! But Jesus wasn't afraid. He didn't bat an eye. After all, even demons bowed down to Him! Read about it in Mark 5:1–20.

Think About It
- A wild man who can tear chains apart is running toward you! How would you feel? What would you do?
- Why did the Gerasenes ask Jesus to leave? Why would they rather have had a demonic strongman around than Jesus?
- What's more important to God—one man or two thousand pigs? Why? How can you tell?

Go Deeper
Read Matthew 19:21; Mark 5:21–6:56; Luke 12:16–40; Ephesians 4:32; Philippians 2:1–16.

Prayer Starter
It can be tough showing love to people who seem weird, mean, or unpleasant, but they probably need love badly. Talk to God about when you find it hard to love. Ask Him to help you show compassion to everyone, as Jesus did.

Facts and Fun
Jews today who "keep kosher" (keep the Jewish laws about food) do not eat pork because it is forbidden in the Law of Moses. This was also true in Jesus' time. Pigs were considered "unclean" animals. So the Gerasenes must have been Gentiles. Even they probably didn't eat those pigs after they'd drowned though!

Coming Up Next:
Things aren't really as they seem. Can you break the law but actually *not* break the law? Find out . . . next time!

CLEAN HANDS, DIRTY HEARTS

Is it possible? Did Jesus actually do something wrong? It depends who you're listening to. Get the scoop in Mark 7:1–23.

Think About It

- God gave us His laws to protect us. Parents make rules to protect their children, too. Imagine you heard a parent tell a child not to run into the street. If the child *walked* into the street would he or she be disobeying? What matters more: what a rule says or what it means? Who in this passage understood the meaning of God's laws?
- Why do you think the Pharisees kept the rules? What did they hope to gain from it? What's wrong with caring more about how you look outside than about how you are inside?
- The Pharisees were phony through and through. Jesus called them hypocrites. Why is it important to be the same inside and out? Name three ways you can be that way.

Go Deeper
Read Matthew 23:1–29; Mark 7:24–8:38; Luke 13:10–17.

Prayer Starter
Think about what it means to be totally real, totally phony, or somewhere in between. Talk to God about it and how you can let others see the *real* you. That's the best they can see!

Facts and Fun
In ancient Greek theatre, a "hypocrite" was a person who acted on stage with a mask. Hypocrites are still actors!

Coming Up Next:
Five men meet on a mountain, but later only three of them make it back down. What's up? Find out . . . next time!

GRUDGES NOT ALLOWED!

What if you owed so much money that it would take the rest of your life to pay it back? Read Matthew 17:1–8 and 18:21–35.

Think About It

• What would you think if your best friend suddenly started glowing? If a cloud spoke and said to listen to him or her, would you? How would you treat your friend after that? Why?

• If this Jesus, whom you saw transformed, said to forgive others, what would you do? Why?

• How is our sin like the unforgiving servant's debt? When other people wrong or hurt you, how is your response like the unforgiving servant? Unlike him?

Go Deeper

Read 2 Chronicles 7:14; Matthew 6:13–15; 16:18–27; 17:9–18:20; Luke 17:3–4; 23:34; Colossians 3:13.

Prayer Starter

The Bible says we need to forgive others to be forgiven. Talk to God about this. Tell Him how you feel about forgiving others and how it feels when someone forgives you. Talk to Him about who you need to forgive and why. Thank Him for forgiving you when you messed up.

Facts and Fun

Depending on the translation, the Bible says we should forgive another person either seventy-seven or seventy times seven times. How many would that be? Seven is a perfect number in the Bible. Jesus meant that we should forgive *every* time!

Coming Up Next:

Everyone's in an uproar! That kid is going at it again! Stand back! Why? Find out . . . next time!

DO YOU REALLY BELIEVE?

The disciples can't handle a *really* wild kid, so Jesus is called in! What's *with* the kid? Find out in Mark 9:14–29; 10:46–52.

Think About It

- Suppose you had been there and Jesus asked if you believed. What would you have answered? Why?
- The boy's father was honest. Do you think most people would have been? Why or why not? How did Jesus respond to the father's honest doubt?
- People told blind Bartimaeus to quiet down and leave Jesus alone. Why do you think he kept calling Jesus? If others tried to discourage you or make you doubt God's power to help you, would you stop praying? Why or why not? What three things would help you keep on (for example, remembering past answers or knowing God loves you)?

Go Deeper

Read Mark 9:30–10:45; 11:23; 2 Corinthians 5:7; Hebrews 11:1, 3, 6.

Prayer Starter

Sometimes it's hard to believe that God can do anything or that He cares about everything in our lives—especially when things are going wrong. Talk to God about how you can believe in His power and love, even when you're down and out.

Facts and Fun

Often when Jesus healed people, He told them that their *faith* had healed them. So they believed that Jesus *could* heal them before He did!

Coming Up Next:

What does it take to make you great? Winning an election? Winning an Oscar? Find out . . . next time!

WHO'S THE GREATEST?

Who's the greatest in God's eyes? Is it kings, presidents, politicians, astronauts, sports and movie stars, or church leaders? Find out in Matthew 19:13–28; 20:20–28.

Think About It
- What do you like about Jesus? What do you think the children saw in Him that made them want to be near Him? What do you think He saw in them that made Him say what He did?
- What was wrong with the rich young man's thinking? Who can get to heaven?
- Why do money, power, and intelligence often get people special treatment? Who gets special treatment from God? How can knowing that give you hope?

Go Deeper
Read Matthew 6:24; Luke 16:13–15; 1 Timothy 6:10, 17–19; Hebrews 13:5; Revelation 3:17–20.

Prayer Starter
Talk to God about greatness. Tell Him who you think is great and why. Ask Him to help you see others and yourself the way He sees them and you.

Facts and Fun
If money doesn't grow on trees, then where does it grow? *(Answer: Under trees, because the love of money is the root of all evil.)*

Coming Up Next:
You won't believe who's making a huge mess, knocking things over, and even breaking things! Read about it . . . next time!

WHO SAID YOU COULD DO THAT!

Jesus really stirred up a hornet's nest in Jerusalem! Find out who did the stinging and who got stung in Matthew 21:1–16, 23–32.

Think About It

- If you'd been in the temple, what would you have thought and done when this loving man started turning everything upside down? Why?
- What authority or right did Jesus have to do what He did? Why were His actions right? Do you think Jesus has the right to tell you how to run your life? Why or why not?

Go Deeper

Read Matthew 21:17–22; 28:18; Philippians 4:13; 1 Peter 4:11; 1 John 4:4.

Prayer Starter

How do you feel about what Jesus did in the temple that day? Tell Him about it. Think of times you need the courage to stand up for what is right, just as He did. Talk to Him about those times.

Facts and Fun

Have you ever thought about what a huge effect one person can have? Alexander Graham Bell invented the telephone in 1876. Now practically the entire world is connected by telephone and through telephone by the Internet. If one person can make such a BIG difference, just imagine what you can do through Jesus' strength!

Coming Up Next:

The Pharisees try to fool Jesus again. Can they? What is Jesus' response this time? Find out . . . next time!

NO FOOLING!

A servant runs an errand for his master. A simple errand, really. But danger lurks behind the garden wall! Read about it in Mark 12:1–17, 41–44.

Think About It

- What would you have done if you'd seen what the tenants did? How could they do that and still expect to get the inheritance?

- No matter what they tried, nobody could fool Jesus! Why was His answer about taxes the best one possible? Could the Roman authorities object to it? Could the religious leaders?

- Jesus saw right through people's "generosity" and saw their hearts. Why was the widow's offering more valuable than all the large ones others gave? When you give, are you more like the rich people or the widow? Why?

Go Deeper

Read Mark 11:1–33; 12:18–40; Luke 16:15; 1 Corinthians 4:5; Galatians 6:7–8.

Prayer Starter

You can't fool God about the real you. What do you think God sees in your heart right now? Talk to Him about it.

Facts and Fun

What's your best "April Fool's" joke? In France, children trick one another on April Fool's day by taping paper fish to each other's backs. Instead of saying "April Fool!" they say "April Fish!"[7]

Coming Up Next:

Who would be crazy enough to pass up an incredible, free dinner—and dessert—fit for a king? Find out . . . next time!

---

7. U.S. Embassy Stockholm, Sweden Web site:
www.usis.usemb.se/Holidays/celebrate/april.html

ATTITUDES/HEARTS

Y'ALL COME!

What would you do if you threw a colossal party but no one came? What did a king do who was in this situation? Read about it in Matthew 22:1–14, 34–46.

Think About It

- How is God like the king in Jesus' parable? Where will His party be?
- Why are people who refuse to believe in Jesus like those who missed the party?
- Imagine you're at a fancy wedding feast and someone shows up in muddy grubbies. How do you think the people giving the banquet would feel? What's that person's attitude toward the hosts?
- How do you think God would feel if you walked into heaven with a bunch of dirty sin on you? Why? How would you make sure you got to stay?

Go Deeper

Read Matthew 22:15–33; John 13:8; 1 Corinthians 6:9–11; Revelation 7:14; 19:9.

Prayer Starter

Think about how you feel when you do bad things. Do you feel guilty? Why or why not? Talk to God about it. If you're sorry about something, ask Him to clean up your heart and help you to keep it clean. Then you'll be ready for His feast in heaven.

Facts and Fun

What kind of feast or nourishment is in the Bible? *(Answer: Food for thought and drink for the soul.)*

Coming Up Next:

Jesus does some *talented* storytelling. Why is it talented? Find out . . . next time!

USE IT OR LOSE IT!

What would you do if you were entrusted with someone else's money? Go on a shopping spree? Hide it? Read about what some people did in Matthew 25:14–40.

Think About It
- What would have happened if the servants had risked their talents and lost them?
- Which servant in the story would you have been? Why?
- Why was the master upset with the third servant? (Hint: It wasn't just about money.)
- What "talents" has God given you? Intelligence? A good voice? Artistic ability? What uses of your money, talents, and gifts do you think would make God happy? Why?

Go Deeper
Read Psalm 112:9; Matthew 25:1–13, 41–46; John 13:12–17; Romans 12:6–8.

Prayer Starter
When you meet God face-to-face, wouldn't it be wonderful to hear Him say, "Well done, good and faithful servant" (Matthew 25:21)? Ask Him to help you understand what "talents" He has given you. Talk to Him about how He wants you to use them.

Facts and Fun
Benjamin Franklin died in 1790. In his will, he directed that some money be invested to help young craftsmen get inexpensive loans. His money has grown to millions of dollars and is still helping people![8] Invest your talents for God and imagine the great return on your investment!

Coming Up Next:
A holiday get-together ends in horrible betrayal, lies, and wild stories! Read about it . . . next time!

---

8. William J. Bennet, *Our Sacred Honor* (Nashville, TN: Broadman & Holman, 1997), pp. 308–309.

THE KISS OF DEATH

Jesus makes a shocking announcement. And it's followed by a shocking evening! Find out what happens in Matthew 26:17–30, 47–50, 55–67.

Think About It

- How would you feel if one of your best friends betrayed you? How do you think Jesus felt?
- What would it be like if, in your most desperate situation, not a single friend stood with you? How would knowing that Jesus has experienced that help you?
- Why do you think the Sanhedrin had so much trouble finding even *false* evidence against Jesus? Has anyone ever lied about you? How did you feel?

Go Deeper

Read Exodus 20:16; Proverbs 19:5; Matthew 5:43–45; 20:18; 26:31–46; Romans 12:19–21.

Prayer Starter

Jesus understands how it hurts to be betrayed or lied about. If that has happened to you, tell Him about it and ask Him to help you forgive those who hurt you. Also pray that God will keep you from lying about or betraying someone else, even by mistake.

Facts and Fun

Did you know that Jesus washed all the disciples' feet—even Judas'? (See John 13:1–5, 10–11, 21.) Jesus knew that Judas would betray him, but He washed his feet anyway. What a good example for us!

Coming Up Next:

A lovely scent causes a big stink, and sends a traitor on a deadly mission. Read about it . . . next time!

THE TEST OF FRIENDSHIP

Things are heating up for Jesus. An angry mob is gathering. How will Jesus' friends handle it? Find out in Mark 14:1–11, 44–50, 66–72.

Think About It

- If you had been with Jesus during all these events, how would you have felt?
- The woman showed love for Jesus, even though others disapproved. How is her behavior different from Judas'? She *gave* something valuable. He *got* something valuable—30 silver coins. Which person would you rather be like? Why?
- The disciples were afraid and ran away. They had promised to stick by Jesus. But swords and clubs changed their minds. Why do you think Peter denied Jesus three times? How do you think he felt afterwards? What could make *you* afraid to stand up for Jesus? Why?

Go Deeper

Read Mark 13:13; 14:51–65; Luke 7:47; John 15:19–21; Revelation 2:10.

Prayer Starter

Jesus can give you the courage you need to be loyal to Him. Pray for strength to stand up for Him. Ask Him to help you know that He's worth it.

Facts and Fun

The perfume the woman used on Jesus was worth about a year's salary. Judas' silver for betraying Jesus was worth about four month's wages.

Coming Up Next:

What happened to Jesus? Did the Devil finally defeat Him? No way? Well, what did happen then? Find out . . . next time!

THE DARKEST DAY AND THE BRIGHTEST DAWN

Arrested, deserted, beaten, mocked . . . was all hope lost for Jesus? Find out in Matthew 27:11–14, 27–31, 57–61; 28:1–10.

Think About It

- Jesus was innocent. He died to pay the penalty for everyone else's sins. He did it so we could be forgiven and have a relationship with God. What would make you willing to suffer in someone else's place? How do you feel knowing Jesus gave His life for you?
- Knowing He would die for them, how do you think Jesus felt when soldiers spit on Him, hit Him, and crowned Him with thorns? Was it easy for Him? Why or why not?
- It seemed the bad guys had won. Wrong! Imagine being with Mary at the empty tomb. What would that morning have been like? How would you have felt?

Go Deeper

Read Isaiah 53:3–12; Matthew 27:32–56; 28:11–20; John 10:14–18; 17:1–2; 19:10–11.

Prayer Starter

Thank Jesus for suffering and dying so that you can be forgiven. Talk to Him about what that means to you.

Facts and Fun

Signs that Jesus is God:

At birth: angels, star

At death: darkness, earthquake, graves opened, people resurrected

At baptism: dove, voice from heaven

During ministry: miracles, transfiguration

Afterward: His own resurrection

Coming Up Next:

God the Father has the most fantastic gift in the history of the world for you. Find out what it is . . . next time!

TEARING OPEN THE GIFT

Jesus is condemned to die. An old saying goes, "When God closes a door, He opens a window." What window did God open? What does it have to do with you? Read Mark 15:1, 15, 33–47; 16:1–7.

Think About It

- How would you have felt standing with the women watching Jesus die? Why?
- The temple curtain was torn from top to bottom, not bottom to top. Nobody climbed up and tore it. God did it! The curtain had separated sinful people from the holy place where God lived among them in a special way. Why do you think God tore it open just then? How did Jesus open the way for us to get close to God?
- Why is God stronger than death? Why do you think it was important for Jesus to rise from the dead?

Go Deeper

Read Mark 15:16–32; John 14:19; Colossians 1:18; Hebrews 9:1–12, 23–28.

Prayer Starter

How do you feel knowing that the door is wide open for you to get close to the God of the universe? Pretty cool, huh? Talk to Him about it.

Facts and Fun

According to Josephus, an early Jewish historian, the curtain that tore when Jesus died was four inches thick. If horses had been tied to either side, they couldn't have pulled it apart![9]

Coming Up Next:

Jesus wins! The church begins! But now there's trouble brewing among believers. Find out why . . . next time!

---

9. New American Standard *Ryrie Study Bible*, Expanded Edition, (Chicago, Moody Press, 1995), page 131.

1 & 2 CORINTHIANS

Some of the most famous and beautiful words of Scripture are in these books. See how many you can recognize. But hold on to your seat! You're also going to read about strange languages, talking eyeballs, true love, and . . . baby food!

Do you like getting e-mail and letters? The people in the first century didn't have the Internet or mail. Friends carried letters instead. The apostle Paul traveled hundreds of miles telling people about Jesus. He started many churches and is like a loving father to them. Paul feels responsible for helping these new Christians stay strong in their faith. So he writes them letters.

Two letters go to the church in Corinth, a city in Greece. In Paul's first letter to the Corinthians, he talks about getting along, staying away from sin, and treating each other properly. He also teaches about worship, giving, and the Resurrection.

By the time he writes the second letter later that same year, rumors are spreading. He has to defend himself from them.

From persecutor to preacher in one dazzling day

The apostle Paul wrote these letters in A.D. 55. Before he became a believer, his name was Saul and he sent Christians to prison! One day a bolt of light knocked him to the ground, and God spoke to him from heaven. After that, Saul was never the same. He became the main missionary to the non-Jews, or Gentiles. (If you want to know more about Paul, read his story in the book of Acts.)

Who needs to grow up and listen to the truth?

The Corinthians started letting nonbelievers lead them into sin. Paul wants to get them back on track. He urges them to stop sinning and grow up in their faith and, in the second letter, he sets things straight about the lies that false teachers are spreading about him. Paul encourages the Corinthians to stay strong and stop listening to false teachers. These messages are important for us, too, because sin is all around us today.

STOP THE FIGHTING!

Fights in church! Peter pitted against Paul! What is their problem? Find out in 1 Corinthians 1:10–11; 3:1–11; 12:12–22.

Think About It
- People who love Jesus fighting with one another? What's wrong with this picture? How should it be different?
- Paul was saying that we need to be followers of Christ, not followers of people. Why do you think that is? What happens when we follow people instead of God?
- God wants us to get along even though we're all different. Why do you think He made us different?
- In what ways are all Christians the same? What can you do to help keep peace with other Christians?

Go Deeper
Read Matthew 12:25; John 17:20–23; 1 Corinthians 1:12–2:16; Ephesians 4:1–6, 15–16.

Prayer Starter
Ever argue with other Christians about whose church is better? Ask Jesus to help you remember that you're all part of His body. Pray for help to focus on the ways you're the same.

Facts and Fun
Mouth: "Skeleton, you're holding things up."
Skeleton: "It's not my fault. Talk to Feet. He's running things."
Mouth: "C'mon, Feet, step on it!"
Skin: "Don't sweat it, I've got everything covered."
Arm: "What makes you so great? I'll give them a hand."
Muscles: "You can't make a move without me."
Brain: "Look, I'm the brains behind it."
Cells: "Let's try to stick together, okay?"

Coming Up Next:
"There's nothing wrong with you *doing* it, but you *shouldn't* do it." Confused? Get it clear . . . next time!

SHOULD I . . .?

Freedom! Yahoo! Some things are right (telling the truth) and some are wrong (lying). Other things are less clear (what TV shows you watch). Just because you *can* do something, does it mean you should? Hmm . . . find out in 1 Corinthians 8:1–13; 10:14–33.

Think About It

- If you think something's wrong to do (or your parents say it's wrong), then it is wrong for you. What can you do that your friends aren't allowed to do? What are they allowed to do that you aren't?
- If you join friends in doing something they think is okay but you think is wrong, should you be punished? Why or why not?
- Why should you care about how your actions influence others? Give at least two reasons.

Go Deeper

Read Psalm 119:45; Romans 14:23; Galatians 5:1, 13.

Prayer Starter

What do you think about the rules you have to follow? About the freedom you have to make choices? Talk to God about it. Ask for help to make good choices and be a good influence on others.

Facts and Fun

With freedom, you can choose to do smart things or stupid ones. Making wrong choices is free-dumb.

Coming Up Next:

Want to know the secret for getting along with everyone? It sure beats getting burned! Read all about it . . . next time!

WHAT'S IT WORTH!

God's handing out gifts! Which one do you want? The best!
Read 1 Corinthians 12:28–13:13.

Think About It

- How can you avoid being a "clanging cymbal" (all empty
noise and show)? The things listed here—speaking in
tongues, prophesying, wisdom, understanding, faith, and
giving—are all important. Why do you think Paul wrote
that they're nothing without love? What could happen if
you do these things without caring about people?
- Read your name instead of "love" in 13:4–8. How do you
measure up? Why?
- How do your friends and family show love to you? How
would you like to copy them? What can you do to show
them how much you love them?

Go Deeper

Read Leviticus 19:18; Romans 12:10; 1 Peter 4:8; 1 John 5:2.

Prayer Starter

How do you think the kind of love Paul described here can
help with everyday problems like arguing or being treated
unfairly? Talk to God about it. Try using 1 Corinthians
13:4–7 in your prayer, asking for help to be like that.

Facts and Fun

When is the only time that love means nothing? *(Answer: In
tennis, where a score of love means zero.)*

Coming Up Next:

What's for supper? Pizza? Burgers and fries? No, but it's
divine! Find out what's on the menu . . . next time!

LOVE

EAT TO REMEMBER

Do you live to eat or eat to live? Find out in 1 Corinthians 11:17–34 what we should remember when we eat something.

Think About It

- The early Christians had "love feasts" or meals before they celebrated the Lord's Supper. Many churches these days have meals or potlucks. What does your church do to help people enjoy each other's company?
- How is celebrating the Lord's Supper different from church suppers? Why is that important?
- Churches celebrate the Lord's Supper in different ways. Although we may do it differently, how does it tie all Christians together?
- Why do you think Jesus wanted us to take part in the Lord's Supper? How can remembering what Jesus did for you help you grow closer to God (for example, it reminds you how good He is to you)?

Go Deeper

Read Isaiah 53:1–12; Luke 22:7–20; 1 Corinthians 9:19–10:13.

Prayer Starter

Tell Jesus what you think about the Lord's Supper. Imagine that you were there the first time. Talk to Him about how you would have felt. Ask for help to remember His great love for you whenever you celebrate it.

Facts and Fun

The loaf of bread Jesus broke was not regular, but flat. At Passover, Jews were not allowed to use yeast to make their bread rise. But the Bread of Life (Jesus) rose a few days later—from the dead!

Coming Up Next:

One day, you're going to be able to walk through solid walls! Science fiction? Or reality? Find out . . . next time!

DEATH DEFEATED!

A lot of people think death is the end. *Is* it? No way! Read the astonishing details in 1 Corinthians 15:1–7, 42–58.

Think About It
- Try imagining what your new, heavenly body might be like. Jesus got into locked rooms without using the door (John 20:19, 26), and He could disappear in an instant (Luke 24:30–31)! What would you like to be able to do?
- How does it help you now knowing that you have great things to look forward to if you're a Christian? What difference does that make in how you live?
- It hurts a lot to lose someone through death. Why is it so hard? What can help make it easier?

Go Deeper
Read Isaiah 25:8–9; Romans 8:38–39; 1 Corinthians 15:20–22; Philippians 3:20–21.

Prayer Starter
Tell God how you feel about death. Pray for yourself and your friends to be ready to go to heaven when it's time.

Facts and Fun
Why did darkness run and hide? *(Answer: Because of the sun's rays.)*

Why was death afraid of the dawn? *(Answer: Because of the Son raised.)*

Coming Up Next:
Death is defeated, but we've still got trouble. Why? Find out . . . next time!

GETTING TOUGH ON TROUBLE

Punched out, crushed, persecuted! How could that make you *want* to keep going? Find out in 2 Corinthians 4:1–5:5.

Think About It
- God doesn't promise only good times. He knows tough times will come. But He's with us even during our troubles. How can knowing that help you to keep going?
- Paul said that even though they were getting creamed outside, they were becoming better inside every day. How can learning to handle trouble well make you a better person (for example, you'll become patient, become a problem-solver . . .)?
- Paul looked forward to being with God. How did that make serving God easier for Paul? What can it do for you?

Go Deeper
Read Luke 6:22–23; 2 Corinthians 5:6–7:1; Ephesians 1:13–14; Revelation 22:12.

Prayer Starter
Talk to God about any troubles you're facing. Ask Him to help you know that He's with you so you won't give up when the going gets tough.

Facts and Fun
In the 1980s, "invisible" gold was discovered in Nevada. It became visible only after the ore was crushed and chemically treated.[10] With God's help you can discover hidden treasure in trouble, too.

Coming Up Next:
Riches galore! All this and more! Who gets these goodies? Find out . . . next time!

10. "Invisible Gold," *Our Daily Bread* RBC Ministries (July 16, 1998)

GIVE UNTIL IT'S FUN!

God owns everything and the good news is He loves to give gifts. What riches did He give . . . and how do we get them? Find out in 2 Corinthians 8:7–15 and 9:6–15.

Think About It

- Jesus owns the universe (talk about rich!), but He became poor for us. How did this make you rich? What did He give you? What do you think His attitude was while He was doing that?
- God planned for the churches to help each other. How is helping other Christians or needy people like giving to God?
- Parties are filled with laughter. Why is it fun watching someone open a present you gave him or her? How do you think God feels when He gives you a gift? What kinds of things can you give to God? How can giving to Him be as much fun as a party?

Go Deeper

Read Luke 12:33; 19:8; Acts 3:6; 20:35; 2 Corinthians 8:16–9:5.

Prayer Starter

Talk to God about what He would like you to give. Is it money? Time to paint a neighbor's fence? Stuff? Ask Him to help you become a hilariously happy giver!

Facts and Fun

When is a church service the noisiest? *(Answer: During the offering, because money talks!)*

Coming Up Next:

So you want adventure? Are you *sure* you want adventure? Find out what it really means . . . next time!

STRONG WEAKLINGS

Talk about adventure! But just how much can one person handle of being shipwrecked, stoned, beaten, and starved? Find out in 2 Corinthians 11:16–30 and 12:1–9.

Think About It
- Imagine a life filled with the things Paul described and then having people say you're not a very good servant of God! If you were Paul, how would you have felt?
- Why do you think Paul boasted about these things instead of about how many churches he'd started or all the people he'd told about Jesus?
- How did being weak help Paul become strong? When you're feeling strong, do you depend more on yourself or God? How about when you feel weak? What makes the difference?
- What are two ways you can rely on God for strength (for example, to help you not cheat or to help you stick up for a kid being teased)?

Go Deeper
Read Nehemiah 8:10; Psalm 59:16; 1 Corinthians 1:25; 2 Corinthians 10:1–11:15; 12:10–19.

Prayer Starter
Talk to God about times you feel weak—like when you have trouble obeying or before a test. Ask for help to rely on Him.

Facts and Fun
Paul was strongest when he was weak, the opposite of what you'd expect. Oxymorons are pairs of words that seem to be opposite. Examples are jumbo shrimp, small miracle, wise fool, happy accident, and small mammoth. Can you think of some oxymorons?

Coming Up Next:
You're a slave! Didn't you know? Find out about it . . . next time!

STRENGTH/WEAKNESS

How are a family escaping from a dangerous country, a person leaving prison, and someone overcoming a drug habit alike? They are all free from their old life and can start over. Freedom is wonderful. Hang on for an exciting ride to freedom!

Galatians is all about Christian freedom—freedom from the Law and the power of sin and Satan. Jesus won this freedom for Christians by dying on the cross for the sins of all people. Galatians explains what the good news about Jesus is, how you receive it, and how you can use it in your everyday life.

In Galatians, you will learn of the awesome way in which Paul becomes a believer and does a complete U-turn.

Paul also experiences a face-off with Peter. The main message of Galatians is that we are saved by faith, not by what we do.

Now listen here, Turkey . . .

Galatians is a letter written by the apostle Paul to the church in Galatia. Galatia was in what is now called Turkey. Paul, the first missionary in the early Christian church, travels from city to city preaching the good news of Jesus and what He has done. Between visits, Paul writes to the churches to encourage them, to answer questions, or to solve problems. These letters are also called "epistles."

Galatians is his earliest letter, probably written about the year A.D. 49 from the city of Antioch. That was less than 25 years after Jesus lived on earth!

Is faith in Jesus really enough?

The Christians at Galatia were arguing about some old beliefs. They thought believing in Jesus as their Savior was not enough and they had to obey the entire Mosaic Law, too. Those opinions were causing real problems. Who was right? How could they sort it out?

Paul wants the Galatians to understand how the good news of Jesus' death and resurrection is all they need to believe in. He wants them to know that Jesus freed them from sin, Satan, and everything that goes against this good news.

LISTEN TO MY SIDE OF THE STORY!

Ever been told to "tell your side of the story" when you are in an argument with someone? Read Galatians 1:6–2:2, 7–8 to find out how Paul defended himself in an argument with an entire church.

Think About It

- Paul is telling the Galatians to believe the gospel just as it's written. Do you believe everything in the gospel? What part of Paul's argument would convince you?
- The gospel is the good news that Jesus' death paid for the sins of all people so that they can be forgiven and live forever in heaven some day. Jesus told Paul to preach this good news. How would you feel with Jesus behind you telling you to go for it? (Courageous? Determined? Scared?) Why?
- What's your favorite part of the gospel message about Jesus? Why? Name three things it helps you do (for example, forgive others, tell others like Paul did).

Go Deeper

Read John 3:16; Acts 15:1–21; Romans 10:9–13; Titus 3:5–7.

Prayer Starter

Tell God what the gospel means to you. If there are things in it that you have trouble believing, talk to Him about them.

Facts and Fun

What kind of ears do you find on a train? *(Answer: Engineers)*

Coming Up Next:

Have you ever tried to tell someone something and felt like you were talking to a stone wall? Learn how Paul tried talking some sense into "stone walls" . . . next time!

ACTING LIKE FOOLS

Talk about upset! What got Paul's goat? Ever have someone do something so foolish that you wondered what happened to his brain? Read Galatians 3:1–14; 5:1–9 to find out how Paul felt about the Galatians.

Think About It

- How had the Galatians gone backwards?
- What kind of "laws" do Christians today sometimes think you have to keep to make it to heaven? Do any of these laws help you get there? Why or why not?
- Being good or doing everything right is important but it won't save you from the results of your sin. Believing in Jesus is the only thing that does that. How does that take the pressure off needing to never make mistakes?

Go Deeper

Read Romans 3:22–24; Galatians 4:1–31; Ephesians 2:8.

Prayer Starter

Read John 14:6. Think of the message of this Bible verse as you say your prayers today. How does it make you feel? Tell God about it.

Facts and Fun

Josh was learning the books of the New Testament. "I'll never get these right!" he said. "I just can't remember what comes after 2 Corinthians!"

"Gotta eat popcorn," Mom answered.

"Will that make my brain work better?" he asked.

Mom laughed and said, "Probably not, but it can help you remember Galatians, Ephesians, Philippians, Colossians—G–E–P–C."

Coming Up Next:

Are you dead or alive, an alien or a citizen? Learn how to change from one to the other . . . next time!

EPHESIANS, PHILIPPIANS, & COLOSSIANS

Put on your armor! Run the most important race ever! Win! These three letters from Paul are full of encouragement and advice for the churches in Ephesus, Philippi, and Colosse—and to all Christians everywhere.

Paul spent over three years with the church in the seaport of Ephesus, the most important city in western Asia Minor (modern Turkey). His letter to the Ephesians answers the question, "Why am I here?" The answer may surprise you. It has to do with living as Christians, putting on God's armor, and living forever. Interested? Read on.

In Philippians you get to run a race—but keep your eye on the prize! It also tells about what it means to be joyful, humble, and satisfied.

In Colossians you will meet Someone who is more important than anything or anyone. He created everything and everything was created for Him.

Excuse me, prisoner #45723; do you have a stamp?

These three books were written by the missionary apostle Paul to the churches. Paul wrote them during the years A.D. 60–61 while he was a prisoner in Rome. That's why they're sometimes called the Prison Epistles.

Out with the old, in with the new!

Paul wants the Ephesians to think of themselves as brand new people. When they became believers in Jesus Christ, they changed completely, almost like caterpillars become butterflies. Paul wants them to know about all the good things that Jesus gives them. In Ephesians he tells them to think well of each other and encourage one another.

Even prisoners need money, and the Philippians came through for Paul. In this letter he thanks them for being generous and warns them about false teachers who are spreading lies.

Some false teachers in Colosse were saying they had special knowledge on how to be forgiven and live forever with God. Paul wants to show the believers that they have everything they need in Jesus. Colossians explains how nothing we can do or say can add to what Jesus has already done for us.

DEAD OR ALIVE

Cowboy movies often have wanted posters with pictures of the bad guys. Under the pictures in bold letters are the words "Wanted Dead or Alive." Paul has a different thing to say about "dead or alive." Read Ephesians 2:1–22 for the story.

Think About It

- Paul says that even though people are breathing and living, they can be dead. What's the difference between being "dead" and being "alive"? Which do you want? Why?
- Part of being "dead" is having bad relationships. Why do you think becoming Jesus' followers makes us more alive?
- Name three ways you can be more "alive" (for example, making up with your enemies).

Go Deeper

Read Galatians 6:10; Ephesians 1:1–23; 3:1–21; Colossians 2:13.

Prayer Starter

Make a list with the title "Dead or Alive." Under "Dead" write some things that can make you "dead" (sin, disobedience, etc.). Under "Alive" write some things that make you "alive" (you could copy Ephesians 2:5). Ask God to keep setting you free from the dead things and to help you do those three things you named.

Facts and Fun

The mean-looking outlaw was boasting about his popularity. They told him he was about as popular as a rattlesnake!

"You guys don't know nothing!" he growled. "I just been to town and seen my picture all over the place. Right under it, in big letters, it says WANTED."

Coming Up Next:

You're a soldier whether you know it or not. You're also involved in a war! Learn what that means . . . next time!

FIGHT WITH ALL YOUR MIGHT!

Imagine you're a soldier in a life or death battle—in the dark! What could help save you? Light and armor! Light helps you see the enemy and armor protects you. Read Ephesians 4:17–32; 6:10–18 to learn about God's meaning for light and armor.

Think About It
- Okay. You're in a dark room full of icky things out to get you. What's it like? How do you fight them? Start with the darkness. How do you get rid of it?
- How are the things Paul talks about like darkness and light? How can you fight the dark in your life?
- You also have armor! What do you think a "belt of truth" is? How can it protect you? What about the other pieces?

Go Deeper
Read Matthew 6:14–15; Ephesians 4:1–16; 5:1–21; Colossians 3:12–13.

Prayer Starter
Thank God for the light and the armor that protects you from the Devil and sin. Tell Him one piece you think you need to learn to use better (Bible, prayer) or something "dark" you're struggling with (lying, disobeying.)

Facts and Fun
Knock, knock! *Who's there?*
Armory. *Armory, who?*
Are Murray and you ready to go?

Coming Up Next:
Do copycats bug you? Relax! Jesus *loves* copycats! Find out why . . . next time!

FOLLOW THE LEADER

Things can get pretty bad if you're playing "Follow the Leader" and the leader herself is doing gross things. Read Philippians 1:27–2:15 to find out about a different kind of leader.

Think About It

- To imitate someone is almost like playing "Follow the Leader." You copy her clothing and hairstyle, actions, way of speaking, and agree with her opinions and ideas. Who do you imitate? Is he or she a good person to imitate? Why or why not?
- Paul says to be imitators of Jesus. What are some things you'll do if you imitate Jesus (for example, be kind, obey your parents, share your things)? How can imitating Jesus be helpful to you and other people (for example, it keeps you out of trouble and makes others feel welcome)?

Go Deeper

Read Ephesians 5:1; Philippians 1:1–26; 1 Thessalonians 1:6.

Prayer Starter

Read Psalm 95:1–7 as a praise prayer today.

Facts and Fun

Why were the ten toes nervous? *(Answer: They were being followed by two heels.)*

What word in the English language is always pronounced wrong even by professors? *(Answer: Wrong.)*

Coming Up Next:

Imagine a race with lots of runners—but only one prize. Who gets that prize? Get the inside scoop . . . next time!

EYES FORWARD

Have you ever run in a race? To know where you are going and to concentrate on what you're doing, you need to keep your eyes forward—no looking back! Read Philippians 3:1–21 for pointers on winning the best possible prize.

Think About It

- Paul said that he willingly lost all things for Christ and that he considered those things rubbish. What things in your life (such as bad language, laziness or anger) would Jesus consider garbage that needs to be cleaned out?
- Think of some things that are really important to you. How do they measure up to the things Jesus values and regards as important? Why?
- Is it easy to keep pushing ahead? Why or why not? How can seeing the bad things around you as garbage help you focus on the prize?

Go Deeper

Read 1 Corinthians 13:10–12; Philippians 4:1–23; 1 Timothy 6:12.

Prayer Starter

If possible, run around the block or down the road today— with a goal in mind. As you run, think of the prize of heaven. Tell God how you feel about His making that prize available to you.

Facts and Fun

Knock, knock! *Who's there?*
Prize. *Prize, who?*
Prize! We're having a party for you!

Coming Up Next:

Who's the coolest kid in your class? Why is this kid so great? Learn about the coolest of the cool . . . next time!

ABOVE IT ALL

Have you ever heard the expression "He's above it all"? It means a person doesn't pay much attention to what's going on around him. Read Colossians 1:13–20; 2:13–25 to learn about someone who truly was above all.

Think About It
- Some of the Colossians didn't believe Jesus was really God. After reading these verses, what do you think?
- What does the fact that Jesus is God mean to you?
- What's more important, following rules or following Jesus? Why? Name three ways following Jesus can help you keep the important "rules"?

Go Deeper
Read Matthew 17:5; John 20:28; Colossians 1:1–14; 2:1–15.

Prayer Starter
Think of all the good things you have received because Jesus is God, such as God's love, forgiveness, and freedom. Tell God what they mean to you.

Facts and Fun
If you could travel back in time to ancient Colosse, how would its market be different from supermarkets today? They'd be a lot noisier! In Colosse's market, people argued about their beliefs in several languages, and yelled out what they were selling. And they sold live animals, not dead ones. Quick! Back to the peaceful twenty-first century!

Coming Up Next:
So you think you're alive? Really alive? But *are* you? Find out . . . next time!

GET A LIFE!

You're dead! You didn't know? Okay, so maybe not literally, but when we become Christians, we become dead to the "bad" things and have a "new life" in Christ. He gave us great "new" rules to live by! Read Colossians 3:1–17; 4:2–6 for some rules for holy living.

Think About It

- How would really being dead make it easy to "put off" these bad things? How can you become "dead" to them so that you're just not interested? What could you concentrate on that would help you lose interest?
- Being "dead" isn't the end. You start a new life full of good things. What good things do you want your new life to consist of (such as trusting friends and peaceful relationships)?
- Out with the old, in with the new! How can getting rid of the old (like lies, arguing, selfishness) and putting on the new (like unselfishness, honesty) lead to fun and happiness?

Go Deeper

Read Romans 12:2; 2 Corinthians 5:17; Titus 3:1–8.

Prayer Starter

Write the letters DEAD down the side of a paper and try to think of sinful things that start with those letters—for example, disobedience, envy, anger, dangerous actions. Then write the letters ALIVE on the paper and think of good things God does for you—for example, always there, love, is my helper, values me, everything. Ask God to help you become "dead" to the things in that list and really "alive" to what He gives you.

Facts and Fun

Knock, knock! *Who's there?*
Dead. *Dead, who?*
Dead you know I live next door?

Coming Up Next:

Trumpets! High-flying adventures and low-down persecutions. What's going on? You can read all about it . . . next time!

1 & 2 THESSALONIANS

Trumpets! Flying through the sky! Persecution! All of these and more are found in these letters written to the church at Thessalonica and to believers everywhere.

Many people in the city of Thessalonica lived sinful lives and made fun of the believers. Sometimes the believers were persecuted—stoned, beaten, or even killed for believing in Jesus! Paul writes to encourage them. He wants to praise them for being faithful to Jesus and to tell them that He loves them.

In these letters, you will find good ideas of how to remain faithful to God in a very sinful world. You will also read about the exciting signs of Jesus' return at the end.

What was that about Jesus coming back?

These books were some of the apostle Paul's earliest letters.

First Thessalonians was probably written about the year A.D. 51 from the city of Corinth. Second Thessalonians was written a few months after 1 Thessalonians to clear up some confusion about what Paul said in the first letter about Jesus' return.

What happens to Christians when they die?

All the persecution the people in Thessalonica were suffering made them wonder what death is like for a Christian. What happens to Christians when they die? Paul wrote 1 Thessalonians to tell them not to be afraid of dying. They can be certain that Jesus loves them and died for them. Now their sins are forgiven and they will go to heaven when they die. Paul wants them to know that Jesus is always with them.

In 2 Thessalonians Paul talks again about the signs of Jesus' return. Paul tells the believers to stick with their Christian beliefs and not to listen to anyone who tells them something else. He wants them to work hard and be ready for Jesus' return.

ONE HUGE FAMILY

Persecution, being treated cruelly! Ouch! What do you need most when you're having a rough time? Read 1 Thessalonians 2:7–14; 5:12–24 for Paul's encouragement and comfort.

Think About It

- Which actions of the Thessalonians made Paul the most thankful and proud? Why? How could knowing this encourage them to keep on doing what they were doing?
- Why do you think Paul told them to help and encourage one another? How would doing what Paul says help them?
- How do you feel when you receive encouragement? Like you can take on the world? What difference does it make for you?

Go Deeper

Read Job 4:4; 16:5; Isaiah 35:3–4; 1 Thessalonians 1:1–2:6, 2:17–4:12.

Prayer Starter

Thank God that He is there to help you in tough times. Think of someone you know who needs encouragement— maybe the person is sick or facing a tough time. Pray for that person and find a way to encourage him or her with your words or actions (perhaps you can make him or her a cake or lend him or her a video).

Facts and Fun

Thessalonica was a busy trade center and seaport on the Aegean Sea. It was also located on an international highway and had a population of about 200,000 people. It was huge! But not big enough for Paul to hide in! After his enemies rioted, Paul had to flee the city by night!

Coming Up Next:

What things help you know when spring or fall is coming? How do you know a storm is brewing? Learn how to tell when someone very important is returning . . . next time!

HE'S COMING BACK!

Trumpets blow, the heavens open, and here comes Jesus with all the angels! Do you hide your eyes or do you leap for joy? And what about all those dead people? Read 1 Thessalonians 4:13–18; 2 Thessalonians 2:1–17 and you'll know!

Think About It

- Picture it: millions of people flying through the clouds; angels and blaring trumpets. Would you like to be alive when Jesus returns? Why or why not?
- Many people try to figure out exactly when Jesus will return, but only God knows when that day will be. What does God want you and all believers to do while you are waiting?
- Why does the fact that Jesus is coming back matter? What difference does it make to you?

Go Deeper

Read Matthew 24:1–31; Luke 12:35–40; 1 Thessalonians 5:1–11.

Prayer Starter

Draw a picture of what you think Jesus' return will be like. Ask God to help you be ready for Jesus.

Facts and Fun

What does the forgetful person say about the hereafter? *(Answer: "Whenever I go somewhere to get something, I end up wondering what I'm here after.")*

Coming Up Next:

Who's loyal to you? Your friends? Your dog? Or only your own shadow? Read about a super-loyal person . . . next time!

1 & 2 TIMOTHY, TITUS, & PHILEMON

Imagine being able to look over the shoulder of a world-famous author as he writes. By reading the words as he puts them down, you can be introduced to some real characters—adults and kids almost like you. Well, you can't look over Paul's shoulder, but you can read what he wrote and "meet" his friends.

In 1 and 2 Timothy you meet Paul's friend and helper, young Timothy. He was the pastor of the church in Ephesus. Paul wants to give him some advice on how to choose good helpers. Paul tells Timothy to be faithful and not to be ashamed of the good news of Jesus . . . or of being young!

Titus was another one of Paul's fellow workers. He went on some of Paul's missionary trips and helped Paul organize and lead churches. In Titus Paul gives him advice on how to lead the church on the island of Crete. It's a lot like Paul's letters to Timothy.

In the very short letter to Philemon, Paul asks for a favor. He wants Philemon to welcome back a runaway slave named Onesimus.

Letters from prison.

Paul wrote all of these books as letters to his friends.

Paul was in prison in Rome when he wrote Philemon, probably between A.D. 60–62. First Timothy was written soon after Paul was released from prison around A.D. 63–65. Titus was written about the same time as 1 Timothy, probably from Macedonia when Paul traveled between his two times in a Roman prison. Paul was back in prison again when he wrote 2 Timothy around A.D. 66–67.

How should we live as God's family?

Paul wants his friends to know that he loves them. He also wants to teach them and give them advice.

Paul tells Timothy to do his best, even though he is still very young. He wants Timothy to tell the Christians in Ephesus everything Paul tells him. Paul gives Timothy advice about leading the church and about always teaching the truth.

In Titus, Paul gives advice to old and young men and women. Paul warns against false teachers and tells Titus to keep the church in order.

Philemon gives us some great hints about how we should treat the people in God's family.

WHAT DOES YOUR LIFE SAY?

Picture this scene: You're going out the door to hang out with your friends. "Remember who you are," Mom reminds you. Why is that important? Read 1 Timothy 2:1–8; 3:1–11, 14–16 to find the answer.

Think About It

- Paul talks about worship as a way of life. How can living a life pleasing to God be worship (for example, it tells God you trust Him)? What are three ways you can worship God more by the way you live (for example, you can do things God's way or you can pray before making decisions)?

- Paul has a long list of dos and don'ts for church leaders. Why do you think the behavior of leader's kids can matter? What can that tell you about the leader? What does your life tell people about your parents?

Go Deeper

Read Romans 12:13; 1 Timothy 1:1–20; Titus 1:6–8.

Prayer Starter

Think of the leaders in your church. What are some of the things they do? How do they help you? Thank God for them and pray about finding ways to worship God in your daily life.

Facts and Fun

Ever think about what your grandparents and parents teach you? Timothy learned the scriptures from his grandmother. Peter's grandfather probably taught him how to fish. Jesus learned about wood. Noah's kids learned to build a boat! What have your grandparents and parents taught you? How to fish? The best cookie recipe? How to whistle with your fingers? Good manners?

Coming Up Next:

Do you feel that you're too young to really do very much? Are you? Find out . . . next time!

WHAT DO YOU KNOW!

What happens when you join in an adult conversation and give your opinion? Do grown-ups listen or ignore you? Maybe they even think, "You're too young. What do you know?" Timothy was having that problem. Read 1 Timothy 4:1–16; 6:3–10 for the story.

Think About It

- Some people thought that Timothy was too young to hold such an important position in the church or to instruct older people. How did Paul tell Timothy to respond? Why would that make a difference?
- How can you set an example in your family or at your church even though you're young (for example, do your chores without grumbling, help the Sunday school teacher, be friendly to new people)?
- God had given Timothy talents (gifts) to do His work (1 Timothy 4:14). What gifts has God given you (good at art or music, being a good listener)? How can you use your gifts to serve God and others (for example, paint your Sunday school room, hold doors open for older people)?

Go Deeper

Read Matthew 18:1–5; 1 Timothy 5:1–25; 6:11–21; 1 Peter 2:12.

Prayer Starter

Think of some things a young person (like you) may be able to do better than an adult, such as using a computer or playing sports. Pray for help to know how to use those special things to serve God and help others.

Facts and Fun

Knock, knock! *Who's there?*
Student. *Student, who?*
Stu didn't do his homework. Did you do yours?

Coming Up Next:

Want to be strong? Learn what it takes . . . next time!

WHAT POT ARE YOU?

How are people like gold, silver, wood, or clay? Read 2 Timothy 2:1–26 for the answer.

Think About It
- How would you have reacted to Paul's letter if it had been addressed personally to you? Why? What lessons about "hanging in there" and winning friends could Timothy—and now you—learn from the examples Paul gave?
- Paul warned against false teachings. Listening to them can make people doubt what they believe about God. Have you heard or read things about God that aren't true? How did they affect you? What did you do about it?
- What kind of "article" do you want to be (a vase, a big cooking pot . . .)? Why? Name two ways you can become that (for example, a vase shows beautiful things so you could smile and be cheerful; a cooking pot can handle tough things—like heat—and feeds or helps people)?

Go Deeper
Read Matthew 6:33; 2 Corinthians 9:8; Ephesians 2:10; 2 Timothy 1:1–18; 3:1–4:18.

Prayer Starter
Try using 2 Timothy 2:11–13 as a prayer, substituting your name for "we" and "us" and Jesus for "him" and "he." Talk to God about what kind of "article" you are and want to be.

Facts and Fun
Paul was in prison in Rome twice. The first time Paul lived in a rented house under "house arrest." He was free to meet with friends and preach the gospel. But during his second imprisonment, Paul was locked in a cold dungeon and chained up like a common criminal. This is when Paul wrote 2 Timothy. Paul was probably killed soon afterward by being beheaded.

Coming Up Next:
Titus: "Help! SOS! I don't know what to do!" Paul: "Hang tight, Titus! Rescue squad on the way!" . . . next time!

HOW DO YOU GROW?

The churches on the island of Crete needed to be organized. There were also people trying to stir up trouble. Paul gave Titus the job of straightening out the mess. Read Titus 1:5–16; 2:11–3:8 for good advice from Paul.

Think About It
- "Just say no!" This really is important. How do you say "no" to sinful things like lying, cheating, or gossiping? How can you say "yes" to things that please God, like being kind, honest, and selfless?
- Believers of all ages are to act in a way that pleases God. Name five things that you know please God. How or with whom can you do them?
- God has done great things for you. How does knowing about God's love and care make you want to respond (for example, obey Him, ignore Him, choose what's right)?

Go Deeper
Read 2 Corinthians 5:17; Galatians 6:14–15; Titus 2:1–10; 3:9–15.

Prayer Starter
Write "God's Spirit" on a paper. Try to think of something for each letter that God's Spirit leads you to do (good thoughts, obey, etc.). Pray for God's help in following the Spirit's leading.

Facts and Fun
Knock, knock! *Who's there?*
Titus. *Titus, who?*
Why is your door locked tight as it can be?

Coming Up Next:
Ever feel like running away? Fleeing to a faraway city? Learn about someone who did just that . . . next time!

CHOICES/GODLINESS

RUNAWAY SLAVE

Imagine you're a slave. Your master treats you well but you are never free to do what *you* want to do. You always need to obey orders. Finally you've *had* it and decide to run away. Of course, you need a little money to get along so you take some. Then you find out freedom isn't so great! Now what? Read Paul's letter to Philemon for the end of the story.

Think About It
- Try to imagine what it was like to be a slave. Why would you run away? What could possibly make you want to go back?
- Paul was a friend to both Onesimus and Philemon, and he wanted them to get along as Christian friends. What would Onesimus need to do? How about Philemon? What do you think their relationship would be like after they did as Paul asked? Why?
- Forgiveness can strengthen friendships. How? How can remembering that God forgives you make it easier for you to forgive others?

Go Deeper
Read Matthew 6:12–14; Colossians 3:13, 22–4:1.

Prayer Starter
Are you really mad at someone? Did someone hurt you and then say they're sorry? When you pray today, talk to God about these people and your need to forgive them.

Facts and Fun
We sure hope Philemon forgave Onesimus! Slaves in the Roman Empire were thought of as property, not people. When runaway slaves were caught, they could legally be tortured to death as a lesson to other slaves. Or they could have the letter F (for *fugitive*) burned into their foreheads with a hot iron.

Coming Up Next:
"Two's company, three's a crowd"? Not in this case! Find out why . . . next time!

HEBREWS

Are you ready for heroes, lambs, sacrifices, a court-room trial, and an exciting race? There's no turning back now! In fact, "no turning back" is the message of the book of Hebrews. The letter was written to Jewish Christians. They already understood the system of sacrifices that God had set up in Israel, but they needed to understand how Jesus completed God's plan.

God commanded the Jews to offer blood sacrifices for their sins. These animal sacrifices had to be without sores, injuries, or diseases. Only the best could be offered to God! But the blood of animals couldn't really erase the sins of the people. God is so holy that only a perfectly holy sacrifice could make up for the horrible evil of sin. Lambs and goats were not perfect sacrifices. Who's the only one that's perfect? God, of course! So only God could take away sin completely. That's why the perfect sacrifice was Jesus, God in human form.

There's a lot more in this book. Hebrews will help you understand the exciting roots of your faith and see how you fit into the picture. You'll also read about heroes of the faith who keep going even when the going gets tough. After reading the book of Hebrews, you'll say it, too. "I'm never turning back!"

The mystery writer

No one is really sure who wrote this book. It might have been Paul, but the writing style doesn't match his other letters. Other possible authors are Barnabas, Apollos, Luke, Silas, or Priscilla. The author wrote sometime before A.D. 70, the year that the temple in Jerusalem was destroyed.

Hang in there, people!

Hebrew Christians of the early church had to put up with a lot of criticism and persecution. So some of them may have wanted to turn away from Christ and go back to Judaism. The writer wants them to know for sure that Jesus is the promised Jewish Messiah, that He is all they need to get to God, and that they shouldn't turn back once they start following Him.

THREE-WAY TIE

You think your family's close? Nothing's closer than *these* family ties! Read about them in Hebrews 1:1–9; 3:1–15.

Think About It

- The most important truth to Jews is that the Lord is God and that He is one (Deuteronomy 6:4). Why do you think the writer had to prove that Jesus is God to the Hebrews? Why did he or she quote the Old Testament? Why was it important to use Scripture with these readers?
- If you had lived then and read this letter, what would convince you that the One God is also three persons? Why? How can knowing that Jesus and the Holy Spirit are God help you (for example, Jesus' words are true, the Spirit is always there to help)?
- We need faith to believe in the Trinity—three persons in one God. Name some other things you have to believe when you don't understand, such as trusting that medicine will make you well or airplanes will keep you in the air.

Go Deeper

Read Luke 3:21–22; Galatians 4:4–6; Hebrews 1:10–2:18; Revelation 22:13.

Prayer Starter

Tell God what you think about His being three persons in one God. Talk about your own family relationships. Thank Him for wanting you to be part of His family.

Facts and Fun

Saint Patrick's Day celebrates the man who brought the good news about Jesus to Ireland. He taught people about the Trinity by comparing God to their shamrock. The shamrock, a kind of clover, is divided into three leaves on one stem.

Coming Up Next:

There's a heavenly courtroom and we are on trial! Who's accusing us? Who's defending us? Find out . . . next time!

OUR DEFENDER

In a courtroom, lawyers defend people who are accused of crimes. Our sins are serious crimes against God. Who can possibly defend us? Find out in Hebrews 4:14–5:10; 7:24–28.

Think About It

- Imagine yourself in the heavenly courtroom. You know you're guilty and should be sentenced to death. Your Defender stands between you and the bench. He knows about your sins. How would you feel? What if your Defender takes the blame for you and pays your penalty? The Judge declares you innocent, and you go free. Now how do you feel?
- How does being both God and man make Jesus the best one to speak up for us (for example, He knows what it's like to be hurt or have to obey)? Why do you think God listens to Him? Why do you think it's so easy for Jesus to understand us (for example, He was a kid too)?

Go Deeper

Read Psalm 130:8; Romans 3:21–26; 1 Timothy 2:5–6; Hebrews 2:17; 7:1–23; 9:15.

Prayer Starter

What an awesome thing Jesus did for us! Tell Him how you feel about Him defending you and thank Him.

Facts and Fun

It's against the law in Atlanta, Georgia, to tie a giraffe to a telephone pole or street lamp.[11] So when in Atlanta, keep your giraffe on a leash!

Coming Up Next:

Did God really *plan* His Son's death? Read more about it . . . next time!

---

11. *The New York Public Library Desk Reference, 3rd ed.,* (New York: Macmillan, 1998), p. 631.

A NEW DEAL!

God made a better deal with His people—one that won't ever have to be changed! Read about it in Hebrews 8:1–7; 9:13–22; 10:19–23.

Think About It

- Imagine bringing a small, sweet lamb to the temple in Jerusalem. It will be killed for your sins. How would you feel?
- Covenants are serious agreements. It's *really* bad if you break one. In God's covenants, blood always sealed the deal—something like a handshake, but much more serious. Whose blood sealed the new covenant God made with us?
- Since Jesus was our sacrifice, animals don't have to die for our sins, and neither do we. How does that make you feel?

Go Deeper

Read Leviticus 17:11; Hebrews 8:8–9:10; 10:1–18; 1 Peter 1:18–19.

Prayer Starter

God knows you're not perfect, but you can enter His throne room in Jesus' name. It's because of *His* goodness, not yours. Thank God for giving His Son so you can know the King of the universe personally!

Facts and Fun

The Bible tells us that the life of every creature is in its blood (Leviticus 17:14). Our blood carries food and oxygen to all our cells and keeps us alive. But it's Jesus' blood that gives us eternal life!

Coming Up Next:

The racers are at the starting line, and . . . Wait! What race? What starting line? Find out . . . next time!

FINISH THE RACE!

Want to win the race of life? Have any idea where the starting line is? Find out in Hebrews 11:4–12, 17–22; 12:1–10.

Think About It

- Have you ever run so hard in a race that you could hardly breathe and your muscles started burning? Did you give up? Did you finish? If you finished, what made you go on?
- Why does it take faith to finish the race in this passage— of resisting sin and continuing to follow Jesus? How are the heroes of the faith good examples for you?
- Learning to play baseball or piano takes discipline. You have to practice a lot! What kind of discipline do you think you need to finish this race? (For example, read your Bible regularly, tell the truth consistently . . .)

Go Deeper

Read Proverbs 13:24; 15:31–33; 1 Corinthians 9:24; Hebrews 11:1–2, 13–16, 23–40.

Prayer Starter

How can you rejoice in the middle of problems? Try to remember good things God has done for you. Talk to Him about them. Ask Him for help to run the race of life well and keep on truckin' to the finish line.

Facts and Fun

Everyone expected the hare to beat the tortoise in a race. But the opposite happened. Think the *opposite* of each word to find out the tortoise's secret: Do take down! *(Answer: Don't give up!)*

Coming Up Next:

Are you really who you think you are? Do you know what to look for in the mirror? Find out . . . next time!

In the book of James you'll read about ships, orphans, mirrors, God's enemies, and . . . dragon breath! This letter has lots of good stuff to help you learn how to make the "book" of your life good—both inside *and* out!

When you choose a book to read, how important is the cover? James says that the "cover" of our "books" will show other people whether we belong to Jesus or not. James wrote to Christians who thought that only faith mattered. They believed in Jesus but weren't acting the way He wanted them to. Jesus says that those who love Him follow His commandments. He expects them to love one another.

What about you? Do you want your love for Jesus to show in what you do? Is it enough to tell a starving family that God loves them? Does that make it okay to leave them with nothing to eat? No way! Suppose someone is being rejected and mistreated by your classmates at school. Is it enough to tell them that you're praying for them? Couldn't you also be their friend?

Jesus helps everyone who asks Him. He feeds them, heals them, comforts them, and loves them. Those who love and follow Jesus just naturally become more like Him.

All in the family

James, the author, was the brother of Jesus and a leader in the church in Jerusalem. He wrote this letter to Jewish Christians who were scattered in many nations. The book was probably written around A.D. 49.

Live it out

In the first century, persecution broke out against the believers in Jerusalem. Everyone but the apostles scattered to other areas. These Christians were preaching about Jesus but they needed encouragement. James was one of their leaders before they left, so like a good pastor he wants to make sure they are still growing in their faith. The advice he gives them in this letter is helpful for everyone who believes in Jesus Christ.

MIRROR, MIRROR ON THE WALL ♦ ♦ ♦

Have you ever looked in a mirror and then completely forgotten what you looked like? No way? Well, read James 1:19–27; 2:14–26 and see!

Think About It

- Imagine running to a mirror several times a day because you forgot what you looked like. How silly! Why would James compare hearing but not doing to something this foolish? What could he be saying about it? Do you think he's right? Why or why not?
- How can your actions be a reflection of your heart? What would you like to see in that mirror?
- How long would it take for someone who doesn't know you to realize that you're a Christian? Why?

Go Deeper

Read Galatians 6:10; Philippians 2:12–16; James 1:1–18; 2:1–13; 1 John 3:16–20.

Prayer Starter

What *do* you see in the mirror of your heart? Talk to God about it. Tell Him what you'd like to see and why. Ask Him to help you make it happen.

Facts and Fun

Be a kaleidoscope! A kaleidoscope uses mirrors to reflect pieces of glass or other colored items and make those awesome designs you see in the tube. Its name is a combination of three Greek words that mean "to watch," or look at, and a "beautiful form." When people look at you, let them see a kaleidoscope reflection of God's beauty.

Coming Up Next:

"Well, shut my mouth!" That's what you'll be saying . . . next time!

DRAGON BREATH!

What's so bad that James calls it a world of evil full of deadly poison? Find out in James 3:1–12; 4:1–12.

Think About It

- You've probably seen TV documentaries of raging forest fires and the damage they cause. What were the fires like? What kind of damage can a runaway tongue do to a friendship? How are fires and runaway tongues the same?
- Why does James say the tongue can't be controlled? Why is controlling it so hard?
- How can you prevent "tongue" fires and "tongue" damage? Think of two things you can do to remind yourself to watch what you say.
- What can you do to make your breath "fresh"? When you talk about someone else, how can you make your tongue like a cool drink instead of a raging fire?

Go Deeper

Read Psalm 37:30–31; Proverbs 12:18; 15:28; 18:21; Matthew 12:35–37; James 3:13–18; 4:13–5:20.

Prayer Starter

Have you ever put your foot in your mouth—said something that you wished you hadn't said? Tell God about it. Ask Him to help you keep your mouth shut! That is, unless you have something good to say.

Facts and Fun

There really was a creature with dragon breath—flames and all! It was called the leviathan. God described it in Job 41.

Coming Up Next:

Angels long to be like us! They wish they could get in on our secrets! Find out why . . . next time!

1 & 2 PETER & JUDE

What's it like to do your best and still have everything go wrong? Many early Christians knew. They were trying to live for Jesus but their neighbors didn't like it. They would tease believers, say bad things about them, and even torture or kill them. Peter cheers up his readers by reminding them of the wonderful gift they had received— their salvation. He gives them instructions for living the way God wants them to. Did you know you're a pilgrim, a priest, a stone, and part of a *house*? Let Peter tell you about it!

And Jude says to watch out for dreamers, schemers, raging waves, and wandering stars! They're out to get you!

They know what they're talking about

Before Jesus made him a disciple, the author of 1 and 2 Peter was called Simon. He was a fisherman in business with his brother Andrew. Jesus gave him the name Peter, which means "the rock." Peter was one of Jesus' three closest friends, and Jesus made him a leader among the disciples and in the early church. Paul called him an apostle to the Jews. His two letters were written a few years apart, sometime between A.D. 60 and 68.

The author of Jude calls himself Jude, the brother of James. Scholars believe that he was the half-brother of Jesus or possibly Judas the apostle (*not* Judas Iscariot who betrayed Jesus). He probably wrote this letter around A.D. 65.

How can we deal with suffering?

Peter wrote his first letter to remind believers of God's blessings, to help them understand how to live holy lives, and to encourage them in their suffering. His second letter reminds readers that God's power is available to help them grow strong in their faith. It also warns them to watch out for false teachers.

Jude's letter encourages Christians to stand up for the truth of the gospel when others try to twist it. He wants to warn believers about false teachings that are spreading in the church and to encourage them not to give up.

DO A LIFE SHOUT!

Children usually take after their parents. If God is your heavenly Father, what does that mean? Find out in 1 Peter 1:10–23; 2:1–12.

Think About It

- How do you take after your heavenly Father? How about the way you treat others or how you act and speak? Do they shout that God's your Dad? Who hears the shout? Why? In what ways are you not yet like Him?
- God tells us to be holy. We must be pure, good, and set apart from the world for God alone. How are you different from non-Christian friends?
- If your real home is heaven and you don't belong to this planet, then what are you? How can remembering that help you when friends want you to smoke, drink, be mean, do drugs, or other bad stuff?

Go Deeper

Read Leviticus 19:2; 20:26; Ephesians 1:4–6; Hebrews 12:14; 1 Peter 1:1–9; 2:13–25.

Prayer Starter

Being good all the time is tough, isn't it? God understands. Talk to Him about being His kid and trying to be more like Him.

Facts and Fun

What did the board say to the splinter? *(Answer: You're just a chip off the old block.)*

Coming Up Next:

What should you do if these strange earth creatures ask about your home? Learn the answer . . . next time!

SPEAK UP!

Earthlings need help understanding heavenly things. How can you help? Look in 1 Peter 3:8–18; 4:12–19 for some clues.

Think About It

- How are we aliens supposed to act when we tell earth creatures about our faith? Why does your attitude toward them matter? Don't forget that you were once one of them. How would you want to be treated in their place?

- People can be downright mean when you're different. If people treat you badly because of your faith, it would be natural to be mean back. But you're not an earthling any-more. As a citizen of heaven, how should you respond when you suffer for Jesus' sake? Why?

Go Deeper

Read Matthew 28:19–20; Luke 6:28–29; Acts 1:8; 1 Peter 3:1–7; 4:1–11; 5:1–14.

Prayer Starter

It's cool to be different when your real home is out of this world! Talk to God about earthlings and Christian aliens. Tell Him how you feel about being different. Ask Him for help to treat others with gentleness and respect, even if they make fun of you.

Facts and Fun

What's the best thing an earthling can say to us aliens? *(Answer: "Take me to your Leader.")*

Coming Up Next:

A thief in the night? Does no good to lock the doors? Help! Find out about this . . . next time!

WITNESSING

DON'T MISS THE BUS!

What's this "Thief" up to and why is it good news for you?
Find out in 2 Peter 1:12–21; 3:1–13.

Think About It

- If you were getting ready for the coolest trip of your life
  and your best friend was late, would you want the bus to
  wait for him or her? Why? Jesus is taking a long time
  coming back to get His people. Why is that good news for
  non-Christians?
- God is waiting to send Jesus until more people come to
  know Him. What does that tell you about God?
- When Jesus comes back, it will be suddenly, "like a thief"
  (2 Peter 3:10). What can you do to help your friends and
  family make it to the heaven-bound "bus" on time?

Go Deeper

Read Psalm 90:4; Luke 12:34–40; James 5:7–8; 2 Peter
1:1–11; 3:14–18.

Prayer Starter

Tell God about your non-Christian friends and family. Ask
Him to help them "catch the bus" on time by believing in
Jesus. Pray for courage to speak boldly when you have the
chance to tell them about Him.

Facts and Fun

Why do thieves prefer to work at night? *(Answer: Because
their days are numbered.)*

Coming Up Next:

Enemy spies? Fake friends? Wolves in sheep's clothing? Read
all about them . . . next time!

ENEMIES AMONG US!

Spies in church? Have enemies joined our ranks? How can we recognize them and keep them from leading us away from the path God set for us? Find out in Jude 1–25.

Think About It
- How are these spies weakening people's faith in Jesus? What will happen to them?
- These spies are undercover, but you have what you need to expose them. How can you recognize them and stop the harm they're doing? What can you do to keep from being sucked into their traps and believing their lies (for example, find out what the Bible says, ask for advice)?
- When you hear something that doesn't sound quite right, what's a good plan? If someone says it's okay to do something that Scripture says is wrong, how can you respond?

Go Deeper
Read 1 Corinthians 10:13; 1 Timothy 6:11; James 1:12; 4:7; 2 Peter 2:1–22.

Prayer Starter
Do you sometimes get confused when you hear different opinions about right and wrong at home, at church, at school, and on TV? Tell God about it. Ask Him to help you understand the Bible so you can recognize wrong teaching.

Facts and Fun
The righteous will eat a wonderful banquet in heaven, but the evil will get just desserts.

Coming Up Next:
When you're a Christian, how is every day like Valentine's Day? Find out . . . next time!

1, 2, & 3 JOHN

Have you ever seen those TV programs that show what famous people are really like? John's letters give us an inside look at the perfect and wonderful character of God!

How did John know so much about God? He was one of Jesus' closest friends. What better way to learn about God than to spend all your time with His Son?

John had been around a while. He was an old man and had been a Christian for a long time, so he knew what kind of trouble people can get into! He warns us about letting the evil of the world ruin our friendship with God and other believers. He also talks about how we should show our love for God and each other.

John's letters will help you get to know God better as your Father and close Friend. So settle in and get ready to read about love, light, darkness, and an evil spirit called antichrist!

This writer knows about love!

The apostle John was the brother of James and son of Zebedee. He was also called "the disciple Jesus loved." Before Jesus called him to be His disciple, John was a fisherman. He is the only apostle who wasn't killed for preaching about Jesus, although he suffered for it. He probably wrote these books near the end of the first century, after he finished the gospel of John and before he wrote the book of Revelation.

Why three letters, John?

John wrote the first epistle because he wanted to make sure that believers understand that they have eternal life through Christ. It's full of opposites. See if you can spot them as you read. It also has some great verses that you might want to memorize. John wrote the second letter to warn about evil and false teachers. The third letter was written to encourage a man who was helping God's workers, even though others thought he was wrong.

IT'S NOT MUSHY STUFF!

There's a valentine waiting for you! One of the greatest valentines of all time! Open it in 1 John 3:11–24; 4:7–18.

Think About It
- What's the coolest valentine you ever got? If God sent a valentine, how do you think it would look? What would it say?
- God is love. What does that tell you about everything He does? Everything He tells us to do? How does that change how you view God's "rules"? What do you think their purpose is?
- Love is not just a feeling. It's something you choose to do. Think of three ways that you can show love today, such as helping at home, calling someone who's sick or lonely, or letting your friend or sibling choose what game to play.

Go Deeper
Read John 13:34–35; 15:13; 1 John 2:5; 4:1–7, 19–21.

Prayer Starter
Write a valentine to God, even if it's not Valentine's Day. Tell Him how you feel about Him.

Facts and Fun
In ancient times, people set aside special days called "love days" for settling arguments.[12] For Christians, every day is a "love day."

Coming Up Next:
Quick, shut the door! Why? Read about it . . . next time!

---

12. Robert Hendrickson, *The Henry Holt Encyclopedia of Word and Phrase Origins* (New York: Henry Holt and Company, 1987), p. 330.

WELCOME OR KEEP OUT!

How do you like having visitors? Hospitality is a good thing—most of the time. Why isn't it good all the time? Find out by reading 2 John:1–13 and 3 John:1–14.

Think About It
- Imagine sharing your room with the biggest slob in the world. What would it be like? Would you want to have that houseguest again? Why would a false teacher be a bad houseguest to have? How can you spot a false teacher? (Check out one way in 1 John 3:7–10.)
- How can we help God's work by welcoming into our homes the people who serve Him?
- Hanging around the wrong people can mix up our thinking and lead us into sin (1 Corinthians 15:33). If we mess up and imitate the wrong things, what can we do? (See 1 John 1:9.)

Go Deeper
Read Romans 12:13; 1 Peter 4:9–10; 1 John 1:1–3:10; 4:1–6.

Prayer Starter
Tell God what you think about having company, even if you don't like it. Ask Him for help in sharing what you have with those who are working for Him.

Facts and Fun
In most places sheltering (or helping) criminals is a crime. Many people have gone to jail for it. False teachers are even worse than criminals because they're *God's* enemies!

Coming Up Next:
What could make John faint dead away? Find out . . . next time!

REVELATION

old on! You're in for a wild ride. This is no ordinary book. In fact, it promises that those who read it will be happy! Want to get happy? Listen to what's in store for you.

You'll begin with a view of Jesus so wonderful that John can barely describe it. Then Jesus gives John messages for the seven churches of Asia. These warnings are good for the rest of us, too!

Next, John gets swooped up to heaven. Will he enter the open doors? Wait and see.

Here you'll read about evil creatures with the Devil's power, riders on different colored horses, angels with trumpets and bowls of judgment, a horrible woman riding a scarlet beast, and a really cool rider on a white horse. There are falling stars, earthquakes, locusts, and wars. Best of all, you'll get a sneak peek at heaven!

There's a lot more to come in this adventure through God's Word. What's going to be the end of this incredible story? Will the Devil win? Or will he finally get what's coming to him? Will Christians be okay? Will God finally get the glory He deserves? Read the book of Revelation and find out for yourself!

Visions on an island prison

John, one of the apostles, lived on an island called Patmos when he was older. Is it a resort? No, it's a prison! While John is there, Jesus visits him from heaven. This book is a record of John's vision. He probably wrote Revelation around A.D. 95. Some say that another John wrote Revelation, but most scholars believe the author was the same John who wrote the gospel of John and the three epistles: 1, 2, and 3 John.

Why was this book written?

John wrote because Jesus told him to. The book of Revelation warns Christians about what will happen if they don't hang on to the truth. It also encourages us to keep living for God. A wonderful future waits for those who don't quit!

FIRST AND LAST

Ready to face flaming eyes, blinding light, piercing swords?
Then read Revelation 1:1–20.

Think About It

- Imagine you were with John when he saw Jesus. How would you have felt? What would you have done? Why?
- Why do you think Jesus looked so different from the way He did while living on earth? What does His appearance here tell you about Him?
- What do you think Jesus meant when He called Himself the First and the Last? Since Jesus is the First and Last, and so is God, how important are Jesus' words? Why should we listen to Him?

Go Deeper

Read Mark 14:62; John 1:1–4, 9–14; 8:58; Hebrews 1:3; Revelation 2:1–3:22.

Prayer Starter

Tell Jesus what you think about the way He appeared to John. Do you think it was awesome? Scary? Cool? Tell Him how you would show it in a movie and why.

Facts and Fun

There are so many stars in the universe that even the ones we can see are impossible to count. Jesus created the stars and put them all in their places. God calls them each by name (Psalm 147:4; John 1:3).

Coming Up Next:

Up in the clouds, a mysterious door opens. Will John go through it? How will he get up there? Find out . . . next time!

THROUGH THE OPEN DOOR

A trumpetlike voice breaks the stillness. "Come up here."
What will John find? Read Revelation 4:1–5:14.

Think About It

- While reading, did you get a sense of what it was like in
  God's throne room? Why do you think the elders fell
  down to worship? How do you think you would have
  responded? Why?
- Who was the Lamb that was killed for the sins of everyone? Why do you think He was worthy to open the scroll
  when no one else was? Why did everyone worship Him?
- John saw the same God you talk to every day. How can
  the way you act today be a form of worship? (See
  Colossians 3:17 for a hint.)

Go Deeper

Read Psalm 100:4; 150:6; John 4:23; Romans 12:1; Hebrews
12:28–29; Revelation 6:1–7:17.

Prayer Starter

God is worthy of all our worship and praise! Join with those
who bow down before the throne by praying the words of
Revelation 4:8, 11, and 5:9–10, 12–13. Sing them if you like,
making up your own tune.

Facts and Fun

Psalm 22:3 tells us that God is with us in a special way when
we praise Him. So when you feel sad, lonely, or scared, try
talking or singing to God about how wonderful He is. Then
imagine the Jesus John saw standing at your shoulder looking out for you!

Coming Up Next:

A scroll so important and official it has seven seals to keep it
shut tight! What's in it? Find out . . . next time!

SEVEN TRUMPET JUDGMENTS

A seal opens . . . and horrible things happen! The first six seals have already brought death, famine, martyrdom, and incredible natural disasters. What will the seventh seal bring? (Are you sure you *want* to look?) Find out in Revelation 8:1–9:12.

Think About It
- You've seen through the Bible how patient God has been. Why do you think He finally judges the evil in the world? How does that make you feel? Why?
- This passage talks about some people who will be able to escape the destruction. Why do you think the seal of God will protect them?
- If you knew you could get away with doing something bad and not get punished, would you do it? Why or why not? Who does sin hurt?

Go Deeper
Read Proverbs 10:29; Romans 6:23; Hebrews 10:26–27; Revelation 9:13–21; 11:1–12:17.

Prayer Starter
Though the end will be much worse, many people have terrible problems now. Think about tornadoes, floods, fires, and earthquakes you've heard about. Pray for the people who have suffered because of them. Ask God to keep you and your family safe. Talk to Him about the people you know who don't know Him and how you can help them.

Facts and Fun
What environmental problem closed the Garden of Eden? *(Answer: Sin pollution.)*

Coming Up Next:
Yikes! A raging, multiheaded, fierce-fanged sea monster! Read all about it . . . next time!

A BEASTLY NUMBER

It's creepy! It's ugly! It's the most evil thing imaginable! Why will people worship it instead of God? Find out in Revelation 13:1–18; 14:14–20.

Think About It

- What would be your reaction if you saw these beasts? Why do you think most people will fall for the lies? What would you tell them if you could?
- What will happen to worshipers of the Beast?
- What would keep you from worshiping the Beast or any-one else who pretended to be God or Jesus? Jesus said He would come back on the clouds like lightning and every-one would see Him (Matthew 24:27). How can knowing that keep you from being fooled?

Go Deeper

Read John 17:15; 1 John 2:17–28; 5:18–19; Revelation 12:12; 15:1–16:21.

Prayer Starter

Tell God what you think about all the horrible stuff that's coming. Does it scare you? Does it make you want to be sure and stay on God's side? Ask for help not to be afraid of the future, since He promised to be with you always (Matthew 28:20).

Facts and Fun

Mandie: "Don't you know about the mark of the Beast?"
Toni: "Sure I do. It's sick, sick, sick."

Coming Up Next:

How do the good guys finally win? Or do they? Find out . . . next time!

BRIGHT LIGHTS, BAD CITY

A mysterious, evil city . . . mystery Babylon. What is it? Where is it? No one knows for sure, but it will be a power that leads the world away from God. How is this city like a vampire? Who will stop it? Find out in Revelation 17:1–6; 18:1–8; 19:11–16.

Think About It
- What do you think should happen to such a bad place? How would you punish all that evil? Why?
- Any kind of sin that leads people away from God's love and His ways is like this Babylon. How can praying and reading the Bible help you stay away from "Babylon" (away from sin)?

Go Deeper
Read Isaiah 44:23; 1 John 3:8; Revelation 11:15; 12:10; 17:7–18; 18:9–19:10.

Prayer Starter
After reading about so much evil, wouldn't it be nice to think about something good? Look around you and tell God what you like about your life, your family, your home, or your neighborhood. Be sure to thank Him for all these good things.

Facts and Fun
Knock, knock! *Who's there?*
Orange. *Orange, who?*
Orange you glad the good guys win? Isn't it grape?

Coming Up Next:
You think Eden sounded cool? Wait till you get a load of the new heaven and earth! And find out how this whole story ends . . . next time!

THE END IS JUST THE BEGINNING!

God gives the bad guys one more chance, but that's *it*! How does He finally end it? Find out in Revelation 20:1–21:7; 22:1–6.

Think About It
- With all you've learned about God, why do you think He gives another chance?
- What do you think about the final judgments? Do you think they're just? Why or why not?
- At the beginning, God created the heavens and the earth. At the end, He makes a new heaven and earth. Eden was beautiful, but the new creation will be even better! How do you imagine heaven? Let your imagination go wild!

Go Deeper
Read Genesis 1:1; 2:7–25; Revelation 16:19; 21:8–27; 22:7–21.

Prayer Starter
Think about living with God! No more crying, pain, or death. Nothing to worry about. Just joy, beauty, angels, other believers, and *God* all the time! Thank God for heaven. Pray for friends and family to go there, too.

That's it. We've reached the end of our story—our *true* story! Would you like to live with God forever? Tell Him about it. Oh, and don't forget to tell Him what a great story-teller He is!

Facts and Fun
What will Christians say at the first sight of heaven?
(Answer: "This is the living end!")

Coming Up Next:
Eternity!

Different Ways to Have Time with God

Tired of the same old thing? Here are some ideas for spicing up your times with God and adding a little variety.

1. Invite a friend to a party with just you and the Lord. Have some snacks and study His Word together.

2. Jump rope or shoot baskets and thank God for breath and strong arms and legs. As you jump or shoot, count all the ways He has blessed you.

3. Stand on your head and look at the world upside down. Thank God for everything you see. Praise Him for making the world so interesting and beautiful— even upside down!

4. Go outside and swing by yourself. Talk to God as the wind blows on your face. Thank Him for sunshine and fresh air.

5. Stand by your window on a dark night. Try to count the stars. You can't do it! There are too many for anyone to count. Tell God how wonderful He is for creating the universe and making you to live in it.

6. Paint a picture about today's Bible reading. Thank God that He made you creative like He is.

7. Sit outside or find a quiet place inside. Close your eyes and listen to the sounds around you. Listen to the stillness, too. God's voice inside your heart is still like that. Talk to Him about whatever you want. Be quiet and see if He answers. You might "hear" Him through feeling peace, remembering a Bible verse, or understanding more about Him. Go ahead. He's listening.

8. Climb a tree or find a spot behind a bush or in the

house. Invite God to be your best friend and share this special hiding place with you.

9. Close your eyes and feel around you. Thank God for your senses. Tell Him how exciting it is to feel cold, heat, softness, and roughness. Praise Him for hugs.

10. Invite a younger brother or sister to join you in a special place. Teach them what you are learning about God. Hold their hands and pray with them.

11. Make a poster of all your favorite things. Thank God for each one. Hang it up.

12. Sing out your joy to God. Make up your own words and music or use some songs you already know.

13. God is everywhere, can do anything, and knows everything. So you can talk to Him about anything—anytime, anywhere. Invite God into all parts of your life. Make up your own ways to enjoy your time with Him.

Suggestions for Adding to Your Times with God

Sometimes it's really hard to read just a little bit of something—you want more! Well, here are some ideas for adding to or getting more out of your times with God.

- Read a psalm a day until you have read through the whole book of Psalms. Some long psalms like Psalm 119 may need to be read over several days or even a week. There are lots of psalms, so you can spend over half a year on just this one book!

- Read one chapter of the book of Proverbs each day for a month. Then write some modern proverbs of your own for your life.

- Read one chapter of John each day until you've read through the entire book. Do you have a younger brother or sister? Read some of the stories about Jesus to him or her. Be dramatic, using different voices for different people and putting in appropriate sound effects.

- Read Paul's letters to the Corinthians, one chapter a day, until you read through the whole book.

- Be like Paul—write a letter to someone explaining the good news of Jesus. Tell them how Jesus' death and resurrection saves them and that their sins are forgiven.

- Read through a modern English version of *The Pilgrim's Progress* by John Bunyan. This is a really cool book about the Christian life. It's full of adventure, choices, really bad guys, and heroes—and *strange* happenings!

- Read *The Chronicles of Narnia* books by C. S. Lewis. They are totally awesome!

- Watch videos like *Veggie Tales* or *Adventures in Odyssey*. Along with enjoying them, study the important, basic spiritual principles they teach.

- Memorize a Bible verse each week. Think of the Bible verse frequently during each day.

- Play Christian music CDs or tapes softly while you have your quiet time.

- After reading a chapter in your Bible, read the same story in another translation to help you get a clearer picture of what happened.

- Before you read from a Bible book, read the comments on that book in the *Adventure Bible Handbook*.

Now it's your turn! Add your own creative ways to expand your times with God.

Reading by the Book

Index of Exciting Reads!

Lion Kills Prophet, Spares Donkey!
  1 Kings 12:25-13:34

They Came Back for More!
  1 Kings 17:17-24; 2 Kings 4:17-37; 13:20-21; Matthew 9:18-26;
  27:50-53; Luke 7:11-17; John 11:17, 32-44;
  Acts 9:36-42; 20:7-12

Beat-up Prophet Warns Ahab!
  1 Kings 20:1-43

Speedy Jehu Fools Baal's Boys!
  2 Kings 9:1-28; 10:17-27

Plague Angel Reveals Temple Site!
  1 Chronicles 21:1-22:1

Can't Keep a Good Man Down!
  Job 1:1-2:13; 42:1-17; James 5:10-11

You Don't Give Up, Do You?
  Matthew 15:21-28; 20:29-34; Luke 11:5-10; 18:1-8

John the Baptist—the Waterboy
  Matthew 14:1-12; Luke 3:1-22; 7:18-35; John 1:15-34

Son of God Defies Gravity!
  Luke 24:50-51; John 6:16-20; Acts 1:6-9

Angels and Earthquakes
  Acts 5:17-24; 12:1-11; 16:22-34

Evangelist Driven Out of Town!
  Acts 9:23-30; 13:49-51; 16:35-40; 17:5-14

Apostle Attacked and Beaten!
  Acts 14:19-20; 16:16-23; 18:12-13; 21:27-32; 2 Corinthians
  11:23-26

Shipwrecked Again and Again!
  Acts 27:9-44; 2 Corinthians 11:25

Kids! Don't You Try This!
  Numbers 21:4-9; Isaiah 11:8-9; Mark 16:17-18; Acts 28:1-6

Topical Index

Welcome to the ℱ*amily!*

Heritage
Builders
Helping You Build a Family of Faith

We hope you've enjoyed this book. Heritage Builders was founded in 1995 by three fathers with a passion for the next generation. As a new ministry of Focus on the Family, Heritage Builders strives to equip, train and motivate parents to become intentional about building a strong spiritual heritage.

It's quite a challenge for busy parents to find ways to build a spiritual foundation for their families—especially in a way they enjoy and understand. Through activities and participation, children can learn biblical truth in a way they can understand, enjoy—and *remember*.

Passing along a heritage of Christian faith to your family is a parent's highest calling. Heritage Builders' goal is to encourage and empower you in this great mission with practical resources and inspiring ideas that really work—and help your children develop a lasting love for God.

***

How To Reach Us

For more information, visit our Heritage Builders Web site! Log on to **www.heritagebuilders.com** to discover new resources, sample activities, and ideas to help you pass on a spiritual heritage. To request any of these resources, simply call Focus on the Family at 1-800-A-FAMILY (1-800-232-6459) or in Canada, call 1-800-661-9800. Or send your request to Focus on the Family, Colorado Springs, CO 80995. In Canada, write Focus on the Family, P.O. Box 9800, Stn. Terminal, Vancouver, B.C. V6B 4G3

To learn more about Focus on the Family or to find out if there is an associate office in your country, please visit www. family.org

We'd love to hear from you!

Try These Other Heritage Builders Resources!

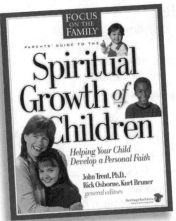

Parents' Guide to the Spiritual Growth of Children

Building a foundation of faith in your children can be easy–and fun!–with help from the *Parents' Guide to the Spiritual Growth of Children*. Through simple and practical advice, this comprehensive guide shows you how to build a spiritual training plan for your family and it explains what to teach your children at different ages.

My Time With God

Send your child on an amazing adventure—a self-guided tour through God's Word! *My Time With God* shows your 8- to 12-year-old how to get to know God regularly in exciting ways. Through 150 days' worth of fun facts and mind-boggling trivia, prayer starters, and interesting questions, your child will discover how awesome God really is!

KidWitness Tales

New from Heritage Builders, these action-packed tales for children ages 7 and up follow fictional kids through real events from the Old and New Testaments. Written by respected Christian authors, these books help children make the transition from Bible story picture books to reading the Bible on their own.

Heritage Builders™

Helping You Build a Family of Faith

Joy Ride!

Use your drive time to teach your kids how faith can be part of everyday life with *Joy Ride!* A wonderful resource for parents, this book features activities, puzzles, games and discussion starters to help get your kids thinking about—and living out—what they believe.

Family Nights Tool Chest

Heritage Builders "Family Nights Tool Chest" series offers creative, interactive ways to teach biblical principles to children in fun, memorable ways. Designed for parents to use as part of their own "Family Nights," these activities will help plant biblical truths deep in the hearts and minds of children.

• • •

Visit our Heritage Builders Web site! Log on to **www.heritagebuilders.com** to discover new resources, sample activities, and ideas to help you pass on a spiritual heritage. To request any of these resources, simply call Focus on the Family at 1-800-A-FAMILY (1-800-232-6459) or in Canada, call 1-800-661-9800. Or send your request to Focus on the Family, Colorado Springs, CO 80995. In Canada, write Focus on the Family, P.O. Box 9800, Stn. Terminal, Vancouver, B.C. V6B 4G3.

Heritage Builders™

Helping You Build a Family of Faith

Every family has a heritage—a spiritual, emotional, and social legacy passed from one generation to the next. There are four main areas we at Heritage Builders recommend parents consider as they plan to pass their faith to their children:

Family Fragrance

Every family's home has a fragrance. Heritage Builders encourages parents to create a home environment that fosters a sweet, Christ-centered AROMA of love through Affection, Respect, Order, Merriment, and Affirmation.

Family Traditions

Whether you pass down stories, beliefs and/or customs, traditions can help you establish a special identity for your family. Heritage Builders encourages parents to set special "milestones" for their children to help guide them and move them through their spiritual development.

Family Compass

Parents have the unique task of setting standards for normal, healthy living through their attitudes, actions and beliefs. Heritage Builders encourages parents to give their children the moral navigation tools they need to succeed on the roads of life.

Family Moments

Creating special, teachable moments with their children is one of a parent's most precious and sometimes, most difficult responsibilities. Heritage Builders encourages parents to capture little moments throughout the day to teach and impress values, beliefs, and biblical principles onto their children.

We look forward to standing alongside you as you seek to impart the Lord's care and wisdom to the next generation—to your children.

Heritage Builders™

Helping You Build a Family of Faith

L I G H T wave
building Christian faith in families

Lightwave Publishing is one of North America's leading developers of quality resources that encourage, assist, and equip parents to build Christian faith in their families. Lightwave's products help parents answer their children's questions about the Christian faith, teach them how to make church, Sunday school, and Bible reading more meaningful for their children, provide parents with pointers on teaching their children to pray, and much, much more.

Lightwave, together with its various publishing and ministry partners, such as Focus on the Family, has been successfully producing innovative books, music, and games since 1984. Some of its more recent products include the *Parents' Guide to the Spiritual Growth of Children*, *Joy Ride!*, and *Mealtime Moments*.

Lightwave also has a fun kids' Web site and an Internet-based newsletter called *Tips and Tools for Spiritual Parenting*. For more information and a complete list of Lightwave products, please visit: **www.lightwavepublishing.com**.